D1785587

MOONLIGHTING
WITH YOUR
PERSONAL COMPUTER

MOONLIGHTING WITH YOUR PERSONAL COMPUTER

AN INSIDER'S ADVICE ON HOW YOU CAN EARN EXTRA CASH

Robert J. Waxman

Technical Consultant
Richard Elen

BLANDFORD PRESS
POOLE · DORSET

First published in the UK 1984 by Blandford Press,
Link House, West Street, Poole, Dorset, BH15 1LL

A Quarto Book

Copyright © 1984 Quarto Marketing Ltd.
212 Fifth Avenue, New York, N.Y. 10010, USA

British Library Cataloguing in Publication Data

Waxman, Robert J.
  Moonlighting with your personal computer.
  1. Computer service industry—Great
  Britain   2. Microcomputers— Great Britain
  3. Small business—Great Britain
  I. Title
  001.6'4   HD9696.C63G7

ISBN 0 7137 1461 1 (Hardback)
0 7137 1515 4 (Paperback)

All rights reserved. No part of this book may
be reproduced or transmitted in any form or by
any means, electronic or mechanical, including
photocopying, recording or any information storage
and retrieval system, without permission in
writing from the Publisher.

Typeset by Graphicraft Typesetters Ltd, Hong Kong
Printed in Great Britain by Biddles Ltd, Guildford, Surrey

CONTENTS

ACKNOWLEDGMENTS

Many people helped me with this book, and I would like to thank those who assisted me in its development. My sincere thanks go to the personnel of Quarto Marketing Ltd., including Marta Hallett, Naomi Black, and Bill Logan. Thanks are also due to Eileen Schlesinger, Eric Lee Smith, Richard Elen, Peter Laws and Fred Barstein. Particular thanks go to Paul Stark for his suggestions and professionalism in rewriting my notes into a readable style.

R. J. W.

DEDICATION

This book is dedicated to my children, Liesa and David.

"There is a tide in the affairs of men
Which, taken at the flood, leads on to fortune
Omitted, all the voyage of their life
Is bound in shallows and miseries"
　　　　　　—WILLIAM SHAKESPEARE

YOU, THE PERSONAL COMPUTER AND YOUR SPARE TIME

THE FUTURE, WITH COMPUTERS

All those rumblings you've been hearing about the Computer Revolution, the new Information Age, are not mere pipe dreams of Utopian revolutionaries and multinational corporations. The computer revolution is here and it is here to stay. The first hints of how this will change the world, our country, and the way people live and work are just now being felt. Every day more and more information flows through central processing units (CPUs), and more computer-stored information is printed by computer-controlled printers. Currents flow, magnetic bubbles change phase, and one more file is created in one more memory, files that translate everything from airline flight plans to exam projects into those long strings of ones and zeroes. In the beginning, computers cost a lot, took up a lot of room, produced a lot of heat, and were owned exclusively by large corporations, universities and governments. But, following the rule that nothing makes progress like progress, it wasn't long before components got smaller, equipment got cheaper, and programming got easier. Very recently, a boundary was crossed. For the first time, inexpensive, easy to use, dependable computers became available to ordinary people. The Personal Computer was born....

ALL THOSE PCs

That's precisely what interests you; and you're not alone. There are a lot of PCs out there: in studies, on kitchen tables, even out by the barn. If you have one, you're either using it for your own business, or wondering exactly what it is you're going to do with it. Sure, you set it up, introduced your children to it, tried your hand at some programming, maybe played a few games late into the night, or balanced your accounts. But what about *all* those fabulous tasks you know you could accomplish with high-powered data processing assistance?

11

Maybe you're just shopping around. Checking out different computer retailers, wondering which, of all these products, line up with your special needs and desires. Though the urge not to be left behind by the personal computer revolution is strong, perhaps you find yourself in a dilemma. It seems like a lot of money, even if they do have a home version of Pac-Man now: you could use that cash to take a holiday, or make some additions to your wardrobe instead. Maybe you're beginning to wonder if there's really an information-processing gap in your life after all. If you're wondering how to do something *really* useful with your PC, or if you're wondering how to justify purchasing a system and what you'll do with it when you get it home, here's the book that will help you come up with some of the answers: how to make some extra money, maybe even some real money, with your personal computer.

MOONLIGHTING

It is well known that a vast number of people earn good money outside their fulltime jobs. No one knows how many of them provide computer-related goods or services, but it's a good bet that "computer moonlighters" are increasing their numbers the fastest, making some of the best hourly rates, and turning their part-time activities into fulltime businesses more often and with more success than nearly all the rest. As a moonlighter, you control what sort of work you do, how much you do, and when you do it—without giving up the security of your fulltime job. Though you may have to purchase an additional piece of equipment or some specialized software, the computer itself requires the largest investment. With just a small investment of time and effort, and this book, you can be on the road to an independent business and an extra income. If things work out well, if you like the work, start to be successful, and have confidence that you can expand your activities, you may find yourself shaking your boss's hand, giving up commuting and setting up your own fulltime business.

MARKETING: WHY IT WORKS

One of the classic rules of capitalism advises the entrepreneur to do one simple thing: find a need and fill it. The pattern of computer use and deployment in our economy provides a definite need that can neatly be filled by someone with a personal computer, a little imagination, and some specialized knowledge and techniques that are not too difficult to learn.

Computers represent an investment, both in money and in time spent learning how to operate them. Many individuals and businesses are not willing to make that investment, don't need to, or are not ready to because they have only occasional or limited projects that have always been done by hand, although at higher cost in wages, time and accuracy. Often, the director of a small company doesn't know anything about computers. He keeps hearing about them. He sees his employees spending hours on repetitive tasks that could be done more easily by computer. He hears that yet another of his competitors has just acquired a system. But he can't find the money, the time, or the opportunity to suspend operations and institute an entirely new method; yet he knows that in the long run, the decision to "go over" to computers is in his best interest. The student, job hunter, or social club secretary down the street could also benefit from some computer applications, but they just can't afford their own computer. Into this gap steps the personal computer moonlighter.

STARTING SMALL

As a part-time computer expert, your first projects will be rather modest. Maintaining a file of resumés, keeping mailing lists, word-processing exam projects and doing tax forms will not be particularly challenging, but the money can be quite good, and the atmosphere relaxed. Also remember, that from the very beginning of your adventure in the world of computers there will be a vast market for freelance writing relating to almost any aspect of computing. As your skill and experience progress, the complexity of your articles and the stature of the publications accepting them will steadily increase.

MOVING UP

As your skill at the keyboard and your knowledge of computers and their applications increases so does the range of your moonlighting opportunities. With some practice and cleverness, you will find yourself able to sell some original software. Thousands and thousands of new programs, as well as modifications of existing programs, are sold every year. The range is enormous. Programs for computer games, for accounting applications, for home budgets and property management, and for many other purposes are on sale right now. The moonlighter with a novel use for a personal computer, and the programming that makes it possible, stands to make a substantial amount of money. If you find that you enjoy programming, you may be able to sell your programming directly to someone who needs to complete a very specific software project.

THE BIG TIME

Instead of running your computer at home for various small projects, or writing programs, you may find that you are more interested in the way an entire computer system might be set up to accomplish a specific purpose. With some knowledge and a little business flair, you could sell your knowledge and judgment to a small business ready to install its first system or expand its existing system. Working as a consultant not only provides a heady dose of power, responsibility and self-respect, it is also quite lucrative. With a little more sophistication and knowledge of the computer market, you may have the opportunity to design and install an entire system and put it "on-line". Although this is the most involved and time-consuming sort of moonlighting, it also provides the greatest rewards.

HOW TO USE THIS BOOK

There is no list of "Ten Easy Steps" that will make you a success in computer moonlighting; there is no easy way to ensure that you will make a fortune with a "hot" new game program. But with hard work and imagination, you can make a significant addition to your monthly income. The most important guideline to keep in mind is that you must develop a service or product that someone is willing to buy, and then make that item or service known to the people who will want to buy it. Chapter One will get you started toward developing the general marketing skills you will need. To ensure that you design a moonlighting enterprise that you can be happy with for a time, it is important that you tailor the information in this book to your personality, the equipment you own or are willing to purchase, and the sort of computer work that you enjoy doing. Because you are doing this in your own time, with no one to answer to but yourself, it seems logical that you should enjoy the actual work, not just the extra money. If you feel you might be interested in establishing a fulltime business at some point, you should always consider how your operation can be expanded, and what sort of associated endeavours you might pursue. As you work for more people, and talk to more people who have use for computers in their businesses, an increasingly sophisticated knowledge of the field should help you discover different (and better) ways to sell your skill and talents. This sort of moonlighting operates much like Tarzan swinging through the jungle: after you've swung with one vine for a while, you'll probably notice another vine you can quite easily switch to, coming your way. In Chapter One, you'll find valuable information about the mechanics of running your own business; information that will make it easier for you to catch that next vine as it comes swinging by.

ETHICS AND MORALITY OF MOONLIGHTING

The only limits to your moonlighting are your imagination and ability, and the amount of time you can devote to it. However, a bit of advice should be emphasized here. Moonlighting, by definition, demands a balance between your fulltime career and your part-time work. While it is not too difficult to find a workable balance point, you should know that you can cause yourself some frustration, and even real trouble, by neglecting to achieve and maintain this balance. You may find, especially at the beginning, that there is less slack in your life than you thought there was. Starting a moonlighting business, even a fairly modest one, demands an investment in time that may eat up quite a bit of your leisure time, time that was previously devoted to more prosaic matters. I will fill you in on some of the prerequisites for different moonlighting areas in Chapter One, but keep in mind that you will need to make a number of arrangements.

Once you get started, you may discover why late-night computing sessions are so notorious. Finishing one last project, or getting that one last stubborn bug out of a program can keep you up for hours, and leave you bedraggled and incompetent the next morning. It is clear that this is a bad habit. Your fulltime job, though it may not feed your soul, keeps food on the table and pays the rent. Your employers pays you to arrive bright-eyed each morning and deliver your undivided attention to his or her enterprises. If moonlighting claims so much of your attention and energy that your job performance suffers, you are asking for trouble.

You should seriously consider the level of discretion you plan to maintain at the office. You may be pleased and excited by your moonlighting adventures, especially as you achieve your first successes. Depending on your situation, though, it may not be wise to ask your co-workers, particularly your superiors, to share that enthusiasm. Some moonlighters report envy and a marked cooling of working relationships, while others find that every lapse or oversight comes to be explained by moonlighting zeal. Many employers like to believe their employees' ambitions are completely satiated by their jobs—running one's own business and making money on the side, can be perceived as a threat, or lead to accusations of being self-important. If your employer feels that your loyalty is strained, he may find it prudent to limit your responsibilities and advancement. Every employer, if he must see his employees leave to pursue their own ends, would like to see such exits draining the company's assets from its lower echelons. You are not doing anything wrong by moonlighting, but a healthy regard for the realities, rather than the pleasantries, of your workplace can help you avoid a whole collection of unnecessary troubles. In terms of ethics and morality of moonlighting, discretion should be your constant byword.

Never use your moonlighting activities as an excuse for any shortcoming at the office. Do *not* use office equipment, such as the photocopier or telephone, for moonlighting. If possible, find a way to receive phone messages by other means than giving out your office number. If you always do a super job for your employer, you should have no major problems.

If there is official, or even quasi-official, concern over moonlighting from the powers-that-be in your workplace, then your situation is far more delicate. Some employers actually have rules against "outside enterprises". If this is the case, you must decide whether or not you believe your employer has the right to make and enforce such a rule. If you are in a position to do so, it may occur to you to openly challenge the rule; naturally, a decision of this magnitude merits very careful and thorough deliberation before you take any action. You should always consider, though, whether a detailed discussion with your boss about your moonlighting plans and concerns might be advisable. If you do engage your superior in such a conversation, you should initiate conversation on the topic only that one time, and you should request his or her discretion concerning its content.

Naturally, work situations vary enormously, and the effects on moonlighting vary accordingly; working for a bakery and an accounting firm differ from each other in ways vital to the potential moonlighter. Those readers working in data processing and other computer-related industries should require only a reminder of the quite serious consequences of conflict of interest, or even the appearance of conflict of interest. If you signed any sort of agreement when hired, carefully review its requirements. Conflict of interest can often be a very subtle matter, but as a rule you should never take any work that would place you in direct competition with your employer. If your duties include finding new business, any client with even a remote chance of interest in your employer's services should be directed there first. Often, a lot depends on observing the proprieties of the situation, to the point of following form for form's sake alone. *Never* take any customers from your employer, even if they no longer use his services for reasons completely unconnected to you or your moonlighting activities. There is always other work to be found, and one should never ask for unnecessary trouble. You should always employ caution, but your fulltime firm's specialized techniques and in-house procedures should, in particular, be protected vigorously. Should the techniques come to be known to others in the field, even if the indiscretion is harmless, it violates a closely held principle of business.

Conflict of interest has led to many individuals being asked to resign. Do not give up the security and perks of your 9-to-5 career unless you are ready to do so exclusively at your own instigation. A constant habit of acting with care and discretion should be all that you require to avoid unpleasantness at your workplace. I cannot provide you with every instance in which conflict of interest may pose a problem. What I can do is urge you to hold it as an important criterion in guiding your moonlighting decisions.

GOOD LUCK

Having been involved with computers as a fulltime professional and as a teacher for a number of years, I know the field is exciting and rewarding to many people. There has never been a time when the resources available to the nonprofessional and the patterns of personal computer use in business have afforded such diverse and lucrative opportunities to the part-time computer expert. It is my sincere desire that this book will start many people on a second career that will make their lives more interesting, their budgets more easily managed, and their worlds larger and more diverse. I believe that after reading this book, and thinking seriously about where your skills and talents lie, you will be able to find a comfortable, exciting and rewarding spot in the world of moonlighting with your personal computer.

Robert J. Waxman

■ ■
■ ■ ■ ■ ■ ■ ■ ■ CHAPTER 1 ■ ■ ■ ■ ■ ■ ■ ■ ■

TOOLS OF THE TRADE

As a potential moonlighter, your motives should be clear to you: extra income, independence, new challenges, the pride of marketing a professional service or product entirely on your own. The actual equipment, programs, knowledge, habits and business matters that may be necessary or desirable are less obvious. You will need a driving curiosity, an interest in personal computers, and the perseverance to get through the difficulties, mistakes and dry periods you will encounter. Aside from these, there are no essential requirements common to the six moonlighting areas I will discuss in the following chapters. This chapter contains information and advice which will prove valuable for all moonlighters. Remember, I cannot promise a recipe for success, and you should use this discussion of the tools of trade as an outline to be adapted to your own situation. Let us turn now to the ammunition you may want to include in your individualized arsenal.

KNOWLEDGE

There is no single asset more powerful, valuable and versatile than the range of knowledge, savvy and "nous" you bring to bear in your new enterprise. In the following chapters, we will see that the value of certain knowledge and the ways it can be used varies considerably throughout the range of moonlighting; however, the paramount importance of a thorough and confidently held understanding of the field you chose to enter is ever-present. Complete knowledge does not have to be acquired all at once, as the opportunities available to the apprentice computer user, in an area such as service bureaus, are by no means meagre. The more knowledge you possess, the larger are your "windows of opportunity", and the more comprehensive are your capabilities.

COMPUTING

You should develop a level of expertise on the operating characteristics of your own PC (personal computer) and, if appropriate, other PCs. Make it your business to understand how the hardware works, how it reacts to various programming environments, and to recognize how things you, and others, may have done could be accomplished more elegantly, efficiently or conveniently. As far as possible, demystify the computer system. None of it is magic; it is a machine, an information machine that accepts instructions. Like many machines, it is complex, well-designed and engineered to be easily used by a well-informed human being. It is not necessary for you to know all the details of binary coding and chip technology, but an understanding of the basic concepts of computing is within the grasp of nearly everyone.

If you are doing any work that will eventually involve computers other than your own, whether it be writing programs or working as a consultant, you must have a firm knowledge of the compatibility of different pieces of hardware, and which software is designed to operate with each type of hardware. In many applications, the question of compatibility must be considered before other questions can even be approached.

For every endeavour you should be able to operate the computer hardware—consisting of a monitor, keyboard, and disk drive—as well as log on, do some simple programming, and easily run prepackaged software. You must be sufficiently comfortable with personal computers to work efficiently, deal competently with previously unencountered problems, and inspire confidence in your colleagues and your clients. This knowledge is gained through practice, aided by instructional material or programs, and through experimentation. If you feel you may be interested in pursuing a moonlighting career that involves programming, take every opportunity to try new programming methods, and re-evaluate your solutions to program problems frequently.

Early on, you should attempt to specialize your computer knowledge. If you are interested in hardware and software systems options, reinforce that interest by guiding your activities in that direction. If you feel more attracted to programming, pursue that: write a lot of programs, explore program constructions, consider learning a number of different programming languages, learn to read and evaluate the work of others. Whatever your interest, always be on the alert to find out more about it. Do not be too cautious about pursuing apparently blind alleys; you never know when you'll find something valuable. Do not be too time conscious or goal oriented; you might neglect to give your imagination full rein. And be careful of specializing too completely: while building your expertise in one area, do not neglect the rest of the computing world; you may become blinded to the possibility of additional ventures.

MARKETING

If I had to identify the single most important factor necessary for a successful moonlighting career, it would be marketing. Marketing is much more than advertising. Whatever form of communication you select to make your services known will represent the end product of a much more involved process. What you as a moonlighter require most urgently is what the advertising industry calls "positioning". *Positioning*, simply stated, means finding a place for yourself in the market. There is no such thing as a "typical" user of a PC moonlighter's skills. The market consists of thousands and thousands of individuals and businesses in different circumstances, with different motivations for seeking out a computer professional. In any business transaction, the buyer and seller are looking for each other. Successful marketing ensures that a large number of buyers looking for "someone" will find you. The owner of a general store can afford to simply open his shop on the high street; nearly everyone will have a need to do business with him. As a computer freelancer, only a limited number of people are looking for you, and in looking for you, a large number of others are likely to come into view. The goal of marketing is to increase your odds in the race for potential customers.

The first step of your marketing plan involves designing your product, whether goods or a service. Does it serve a purpose for a large number of businesses? Can I adjust my enterprise to increase its profit margin by offering a more valuable product, or my volume by appealing to a larger market, or one with less competition? Is my product a necessity or a luxury to those who purchase it? In answering these questions, you should find ways to make your product more marketable.

These and other questions that should be answered so that you can design your product with an eye toward marketability, must be approached with a thorough knowledge of your market. You must know who uses computers, and how they use them; who might benefit from computers but does not now have them; what goods, services and applications are particularly valuable, or presently scarce; which areas available to you are saturated and which are as yet unexploited, and much more.

Only after giving long and careful consideration to the design of your product should you venture into advertising. Once your product has been designed, advertising should not pose a real problem, because you will know, or can deduce, who your customers will be, what they read, where they work, what their positions are, and what will catch their eye and answer their needs. With this in mind, writing and placing your ad or preparing your brochure should be quite simple. Of course, knowledge is the most important ingredient in this process, and the directions indicated here will serve you well in creating and selling your new moonlighting business. Specific marketing techniques will be found in each of the next six chapters.

KNOWLEDGE SOURCES

If you wanted to acquire a used car, you could stand on a street corner and wait for a car to drive by with a "For Sale" sign in the window, or you could visit a car dealer. This same principle holds true when searching for computer knowledge: you should look for concentrations of knowledge.

There are many books now available on all aspects of computers and their use. Many excellent titles are available in paperback at bookstores and computer stores. Some of the more general books can provide you with a valuable overview; those that are more specific treat complicated or technical topics in great detail. You can regularly find reviews of these books in computer magazines.

Another valuable source of knowledge is to be found in personal computer periodicals. Subscribe to a few and read them regularly. They treat a wide range of topics, often aimed at readers of all levels of computing competence, and are the most up-to-date source of information available. Magazines are an excellent source of equipment and software reviews and programming ideas, and ideas for new computer applications. Some, such as *Personal Computer World* and *Practical Computing* take special pains to cater for the apprentice computer user. Systematic observations culled from these sources can provide valuable insights into the market situation at a given time. For example, as I write, computer periodicals and newspapers are providing heavy coverage of packaged programs for personal computers, and the money earned by the part-time authors of those programs. There are also articles analyzing the trends in the distribution channels for this type of program, and their impact on software authors. This is a definite sign that one of the fastest growing segments of the PC market is the writing of programs for resale to a mass market.

I strongly urge anyone interested in personal computers to join a personal computing club. These clubs are an invaluable way to share ideas and experiences with a large number of bright, capable, and enthusiastic computer users.

Remember that books, magazine subscriptions and club dues, if related to your business, are legitimate tax deductions. Keep receipts for all business expenses to ease your tax burden.

Do not ignore general interest periodicals; they are good sources of information that may be potentially important to moonlighting. As mentioned earlier in the marketing section, general information about the market is most helpful in positioning yourself. If you have an interest or some experience in a particular type of business, seek out the trade journal for that field. Trade journals offer a wealth of information about day-to-day concerns of their particular industry, and can help you keep abreast of the latest developments, which are very important to the moonlighter offering modern computer services. You may also wish to subscribe to a business magazine, and should not neglect the business section of a good daily paper, nor any column, no matter where you find it, devoted to the personal computer.

Retail outlets provide excellent, easily exploited concentrations of computer knowledge. You can frequent your local computer store to get an idea of what people are buying and some of the questions they are asking. It may well pay you to be honest with the retailer and let him know that you're there to see where the market opportunities lie for you. He may welcome you as an after-the-sale resource to provide services to his customers.

Of course, there is no substitute for experience. You should vary your moonlighting assignments, if you feel capable of doing the work, simply to expand your knowledge. Make a habit of talking to people in business. Learn as much as you can, no matter what you're doing. Learn from your mistakes.

EDUCATION

Moonlighting success has been achieved by people with little or no formal education, as well as by those holding PhDs. Whatever education you've received up to this point will no doubt serve you well. However, there are numerous specialized educational opportunities designed for the personal computer user. I strongly recommend specialized training to those who feel they may benefit from it. If you are interested in obtaining computer instruction, you should investigate its availability in your area. Educational expenses, of course, can be claimed as a business expense. Here are some suggestions to start you on your search.

If you are presently a college or university student, investigate the computer facilities available at your establishment. Often, the equipment and hands-on experience offered is of high quality, and, as I mentioned earlier, *any* contact with computing should be considered a worthwhile method of increasing your knowledge.

If you are not a student, you may still have a number of educational opportunities. There are adult and extension courses covering aspects of computing, and their resources are often quite extensive. Adult education centres and evening classes often administer some type of computer instruction. Some computer stores also hold seminars, usually of limited duration, and occasionally free of charge.

To judge the educational options available to you, request catalogues, examine advertisements, and check the phone book. University and college registrars, department heads and teachers are usually quite happy to field telephoned inquiries should you have some specific questions. In evaluating any educational outlet offering computer instruction, you should determine the amount of hands-on work scheduled, and the computer-to-student ratio.

GOOD HABITS

There are a number of habits you should cultivate that can ease your moonlighting path immeasurably. Once certain behaviour patterns become habits, you will reap their rewards without having to go out of your way; the habits will become your standard operating procedure. The habits discussed here are those I have found most valuable in my own moonlighting work.

YOU'RE IN BUSINESS NOW

Any economic transaction carries with it a large measure of trust: monies paid will guarantee work of a specified quality; work delivered will guarantee payment of agreed monies; good faith and best efforts will be maintained by both parties; each party will keep in mind the needs and requirements of the other; reasonable requests will be given reasonable consideration; and so on. It is especially important for a person working part-time to avoid giving their client or customer a reason to question the implied trust he attaches to all his business relationships. Keep in mind that business is the world's third oldest profession, with its own traditions and rules, and make an effort toward maintaining the following standards.

LOOK GOOD, SPEAK WELL. First impressions are vitally important in business, and these impressions owe much to appearance. Whether in person, or through your written promotional materials, always put your best foot forward. I recommend that you dress neatly and smartly, shave if male, and be tidy in your personal habits and appearance. Your letters, cards, resumés, advertisements, and finished products should always be professional and letter perfect. Remain as calm and professional as possible in all situations. A little effort toward these goals will make a big difference.

BE PUNCTUAL. In business, time is money. Don't give anyone reason to doubt that what you promised will be delivered. Be on time for meetings, return phone calls promptly, and answer your mail religiously. Respect deadlines absolutely; only in the most dire emergency should you get something in late, even if it's "just a little late". Keep this in mind when making commitments: don't bite off more than you can chew.

BE ORGANIZED. *Never* lose anything, *never* let any promise or agreement "slip your mind". Maintain a date book with plenty of room to indicate all important commitments. Keep everything until long after it may be needed. Start a filing system. *Every* job, client, advertising venue, program, vendor, business expense, and product should have its own place in your filing system. If someone needs a fact about your business, you should be able to produce it quickly. Keep files of clipping on topics of current interest and future possibilities, organized by subject. Sample files include hardware, program languages, software packages, business considerations, and application reviews. Maintain a rotary card index or other convenient listing of *all* names, phone numbers, addresses, and fields of activity you run across. You never know when you'll need to contact someone you may have met months ago. When in doubt, over-organize.

TIME

Every day contains just twenty-four hours. There's nothing in the world you can do to gain any more time. Since, by definition, you will have to fit your moonlighting around a fulltime job, you must make some decisions about the use of your time. If you seriously intend to enter the moonlighting world, you must examine all your present activities to find areas from which you can carve a few extra hours. You must take a long, hard look at your present priorities, and determine whether there is enough slack, and a strong enough desire, to make a realistic attempt at moonlighting practical. Since, up to this point, you've found *something* to fill every hour of each twenty-four, something must be sacrificed to make room.

Obviously, if you work a standard week, you must exploit morning, lunch-hour, evening, and weekend time. Experiment to find the best combinations of time for your personal constitution. Seriously consider setting aside certain portions of certain days as "work time" that cannot be used for anything else. If you are not working on a project during a given work time, find something to do that is necessary to the maintenance of your business. Read the magazines and trade papers mentioned earlier in the chapter, organize your files and records, make phone calls, review your ads or your resumé. If you commit yourself to a deadline, spread out the work in a number of manageable chunks, rather than leaving everything to the last moment.

If you are considering a form of moonlighting that involves personal contact with the "outside world", keep in mind that you will require a certain flexibility in your time allotment at work. The ideal solution is a nonstandard day or work week. If that is impossible, you must use your lunch hours and holiday allocations if you are to meet people during business hours.

A realistic examination of the time you are willing and able to devote to a moonlighting enterprise at the outset can save you the inconveniences of overworking, passing up important assignments, or, at the worst, abandoning the attempt altogether because you really don't have the time. Be jealous of your time. Use it only to your best advantage, whether that involves enjoying your leisure time or getting your work done.

SUPPLIES AND CREDENTIALS

You will need to have your resumé, stationery and business cards printed, and their professional appearance is vital, as they will quite often be your first contact with people in the business world. Typesetting services, though somewhat expensive, reap handsome rewards and should be investigated. Everything should be printed on high quality paper and be reproduced by a professional outlet.

RESUMÉS. This is your introduction to potential clients and buyers, and is, therefore, a very important document. A resumé is a selling tool, and should put you in the best possible light. Education, work experience, and any special skills you have should be emphasized. If you have a track record of any kind in your field, describe in detail: what kind of work you did, who you did it for, what the results were. In some fields, it may be in your best interest to prepare a separate listing of your most impressive accomplishments. The resumé proper should rarely exceed one page in length. Always indicate your willingness to supply references on request. Select as references people who stand as closely as possible to the business at hand, and speak with them about it first. If you're just starting out, references not connected to computing are far better than no references at all. A vast number of decisions as to suitability, character and talents are routinely based on resumés, so give yours a large amount of attention.

LETTERHEAD STATIONERY. Stationery should include your name, or your company name, a complete address and a phone number if possible. A description might be included; good quality paper is important. Ordering a large batch will save you money. All letters and invoices should be prepared on your letterhead stationery, dated, and contain *no* typographical errors and, if possible, no visible corrections. Typewriting is mandatory. It doesn't hurt to have an impressive signature, either.

BUSINESS CARDS. They are an absolute must. Name, address, phone number and speciality should always appear. Have them professionally made up in a standard size. Again, bulk buying takes down the per-unit price significantly. Collect a lot of them, and use your favourites as models. Business cards are often found stapled to index cards, so pass them out to everybody.

THE TELEPHONE

As I mentioned in the first chapter, it is a good idea not to receive moonlighting phone messages at work. You can purchase phone answering machine (a legitimate tax deduction) relatively cheaply if you shop around. However, do not try to save money by passing up the remote control feature; getting your messages at any time, from anywhere, is the primary advantage of these machines. If you don't like these machines, or feel your callers are more comfortable talking to a living person, answering services are available at a monthly rate. However, you can't count on getting complicated messages accurately, and you won't be able to judge your caller's tone of voice. Even in the short run, a phone answering machine will prove less expensive.

PROFESSIONAL SERVICES

If you are setting up a corporation or a partnership, you may want to obtain some legal advice as to the best type of organization available, your liabilities, or any other legal matters that may be beyond your ken. I have included a fairly comprehensive chapter on business considerations, which you might read before deciding to see a lawyer. In those areas of moonlighting requiring a contract between yourself and a client, you may want to meet with a lawyer to discuss how a contract can best be written to protect your interests. As there are no standard contracts in these fields at present, you may consider paying a lawyer to draw up one or two sample contracts that you could modify as needed for individual jobs. In general, however, the legal advice you need to get started can be held to a minimum.

At almost all levels of moonlighting, you should be able to keep your books and financial records without outside help. A simple ledger book, or an accounting program, is considerably less expensive than the services of an accountant. However, running one's own business or earning a substantial second income can greatly increase the complexity of a tax return preparation, thus many moonlighters use an accountant's services at tax time. Once depreciation, home office space, and other tax considerations are taken into account, the reduction in your tax obligations matches or exceeds your accountant's fee.

HARDWARE AND SOFTWARE

Now that I've discussed all the preliminaries, and outlined the optional ingredients for your new business, we can turn to a discussion of the tools that lie at the heart of my chosen trade: the hardware, peripherals, and software from which your personal computing system will be constructed.

HARDWARE AND PERIPHERALS

Although it can be argued that you don't really need a personal computer to get involved in some of the moonlighting activities described later in this book, your expertise and interest in computers will be highly suspect if you don't have the opportunity to gain significant amounts of hands-on experience, for which there is no substitute.

It is outside the scope of this book to recommend a particular personal computer. There are simply too many variables involved to be able to make specific recommendations to a large audience. Numerous magazine articles and books are available that claim to provide guidance in this area, and excellent assistance is available at many retail outlets. There are, however, three major guidelines that you should keep in mind when looking for a personal computer:

• What do you want to do with your computer? This is the most crucial question to answer, as all other questions originate from this simple question. Are you interested in: Writing programs for resale? Providing word-processing services? Writing reports for your clients as a consultant? Preparing income tax returns? Writing games for your use or for resale? Preparing articles for publication? Or something else entirely?

While you may not be able to answer these questions with absolute certainty now, you should have some idea as to your interests and aptitudes.

• Having developed some kind of list of things you intend to do with your computer, the next step is to determine what software systems and packaged application programs will support your plans. This is particularly important if you opt to use packaged programs, rather than your own, since packaged programs are not only written to run on a particular manufacturer's computer, but usually require a minimum configuration of that hardware. A program written to run on an Apple PC will not run on an IBM PC, nor will a program

29

written for a Tandy system run on a Commodore. If you plan to do a lot of your own programming you must determine what program language (or languages) you will use, because different languages are available with different systems. (See Appendix A (page 136) for a summary of personal computer programming languages.)

You may be interested in using a program development system such as a spread-sheet program like VisiCalc or perhaps a program like 1-2-3 that combines file management, spread-sheet operations and graphics capabilities: You may find help determining what software supports your plans at your local personal computer store, or from computer magazines and other periodicals.

• This last step could be the easiest, since by this time you should have determined your software requirements and can now match them with the hardware that supports them. In all likelihood, you will come up with several hardware options, making your job a little easier.

Some of the characteristics you should look for in a personal computer to be used for serious moonlighting include:

• At least a 64K memory (k = thousands but computer memory, being binary based is measured in blocks of 1024 (= 2^{10}) rather than in thousands (= 10^3); K is often used for Kilobytes = 1024 bytes and 1K memory is 1024 bytes and not 1000 bytes; a byte is equivalent to about one character). Some of the more comprehensive programming systems require a larger memory.

• A standard typwriter keyboard with a good feel. It is important that you try out any keyboard before buying.

• At least one disk drive. Invariably, you will soon move to two disk drive for ease of operation.

• A separate monitor for your computer. The quality of television screens, while adequate for television viewing, is usually not sufficient for computer use and will cause frustration and possibly eyestrain. You may also find the miniature monitor screens now on the market too small and impractical.

• The monitor display should present 80 columns and 24 rows. The personal computer field is changing so rapidly that any listing of computer hardware and prices will, in a short time, be obsolete. However, it may be useful to list some of the more popular personal computers now on the market if only for purposes. of comparison.

IBM PC. This is an example of a totally unbundled system—you assemble the hardware from an impressive array of separately available 64K memory, keyboard, and two 320K disk drives, mono-chrome display, interface, and basic dot-matrix printer, including cable.

Apple IIe. This replaces the Apple II Plus and comes with 64K memory as standard, with an optional 64K memory expansion. The basic starter system includes the console, monitor, and a 140K disk drive, but not a printer, which will add to the cost. An 80-column monitor display is available for an additional cost.

TRS-80, Model 4. This replaces TRS-80 Model III and has a built-in 24 by 80 display, with a 64K memory, expandable to 128K with two 184K disk drives and a 50 character per second (cps) is extra. A 5 million character "hard" disk is also available.

Commodore 64. This computer is considered to be less powerful than those mentioned above, but has word processing and account-ing software available. The basic 64K (not expandable) system, with keyboard, lists for £200, a disk drive lists at £299, and a printer lists at close to £230.

Sinclair QL. This new, low price system, with micro-drive and software inclusive packages is also well worth investigating.

• In order to ensure that you are keeping up with the rapidly changing and increasing range of hardware, with the inevitable range of discounted prices, you must check out the array of computer, magazines now available (See Appendix C (page 141)).

OTHER COSTS

In addition to the basic computer purchase price, you must allow for maintenance costs. These are generally purchased through a main-tenance contract with the vendor who sold you the system, usually costing about 10% of the computer purchase price per year. Main-tenance can be contracted on an on-site basis, or on a carry-in plan. In addition to maintenance by the vendor that sold you the system, maintenance is available from third-party suppliers. If you purchase your computer components from several suppliers, you may have to engage a third-party maintenance supplier to service your system, as a particular vendor may not be willing to service components that he does not sell. Also, supplies such as paper, diskettes, and printer ribbons should be budgeted, along with a suitable table and filing cabinets.

It should be noted here that many of the aforementioned equipment purchase prices are subject to substantial discounts, and shopping for the best buy is definitely recommended.

SOFTWARE AND PROGRAMS

In addition to the computer and the associated peripherals such as printers and disk drives, you will need software to drive your system. This software can be classified into several categories including:

- Operating systems
- Applications programs
- Application development programs
- Programming languages and compilers
- Communications programs
- Utilities

OPERATING SYSTEMS are almost invariably supplied by the hardware manufacturer and are included in your computer system. Your computer will not run without one. Typical operating systems are the PC-DOS systems supplied with the IBM PC and the TRSDOS supplied with the Tandy models. An operating system is a group of programs that direct the flow of data in and out of the computer memory to the peripherals and also control interaction between programs. Memory is allocated by the operating system, and the actual operation of hardware such as keyboards is controlled. Some of the more advanced operating systems include compilers and utilities. You may purchase operating systems to run on your computer that will augment those originally supplied. The most popular operating system, if measured by the number of applications programs available to run under it, is CP/M.

Although moving to another operating system could provide some benefits, like the ability to access more programs with CP/M, users generally stay with the hardware manufacturer's system, particularly when the user is new to personal computers.

APPLICATIONS PROGRAMS are the software that do the job you are interested in. These cover the thousands of classes of programs running on the computer, including accounting programs, inventory control, payroll, mail lists, scientific calculations, billing, and the programs you write to do a specific task. Naturally, these programs can be purchased, which should be your first choice, or written to meet your particular requirements.

How do you select the proper packaged application program? The first task is to carefully determine your system requirements. How many people will be paid by the payroll system? How many general ledger accounts will be used? Is the accounts receivable system a balance or item forward operation? What are the reporting formats desired? Having answered questions on system requirements, the next step is to answer the following questions:

- How well do the capabilities of the package meet your needs?
- Will the program run on the computer you have, or plan to purchase?
- How flexible is the package—can changes be made easily to meet changing conditions?
- Is source code available to allow changes to be made?
- How difficult is the package to install? Are there new forms?
- How easy will the system be to use?
- Is the documentation adequate?
- What is the after-sales support like?
- When was the program developed, and how many have been sold?
- What is the purchase price?

APPLICATION DEVELOPMENT PROGRAMS assist you in writing programs to meet a specific set of requirements. These are extremely popular, and examples of this class are the spread-sheet programs, like VisiCalc and all its clones, database systems, and programs that combine several functions such as spread-sheets, graphics and database activities, typified by 1-2-3. Despite advertising claims to the contrary, you should have some knowledge of information systems to use these packages effectively, although for extremely simple applications, a beginner might have some success.

You should look into this class of software when a packaged program doesn't exactly meet your needs and you don't want to go to the expense and trouble of writing a program from scratch. The spread-sheet packages work well where the application is largely numeric and in tabular form, such as balance sheets or profit-and-loss statements, and a relationship can be established between rows and columns. Where there is a great deal of file manipulation, and you wish to retrieve data by varied criteria, a database system should be explored. Database systems require two disk drives for efficient operation, along with at least 64K memory. Some questions to be asked about your application before investigating a database system are:

- How complicated are the retrieval criteria?

- What is the format of the data to be manipulated?
- What is the volume of data to be stored?
- What kind of output do I want?

Armed with answers to these questions, you can match the database parameters with your needs.

PROGRAMMING LANGUAGES AND COMPILERS. If you choose to write your own programs from scratch, you will need a programming language that runs on your computer. Virtually all personal computers today come with some form of BASIC as the native programming language. This is an excellent tool for beginners, but there are other languages that have advantages over BASIC. Some programming languages require a compiler to translate your code into a form the computer can recognize. Appendix A (page 136) covers personal computer programming languages in some detail.

COMMUNICATIONS PROGRAMS. This is a class of software that allows your computer to communicate over telephone lines with other computer systems. These are very specialized programs, and will, among their many capabilities, permit you to transfer files, access databases, automatically log on to predefined systems and provide certain security features for your files. Some of the more advanced program-development systems incorporate communications capabilities in their packages. (In addition to the communications program, you will need a piece of hardware called a *modem* to interface your computer to the telephone network.) Some of the questions to answer in evaluating a communications package are:

- Will it run on my computer?
- What are the transmission speeds? (300 bps-bits per sec—is minimum.)
- Are there limitations to file transfer size?
- Does it verify the accuracy of the transmission?
- Are there automatic log-on procedures?

UTILITIES. The last type of software performs functions within your system that make its operation more efficient and ease your interface with the system. Typical are the print spoolers that copy a file to your disk drive or allocate separate print buffers in memory, set up the printing routine, and then allow your computer to use that file's memory area for more productive tasks. Another example is the electronic disk, which simulates disk files in your memory for very fast operations, at the expense, of course, of capturing memory for its operation. This class of program is most useful for heavy users of personal computers.

ACQUISITION ALTERNATIVES

There are three basic ways of acquiring personal computers: 1) outright purchase (the most common); 2) leasing, usually for several years; and 3) short-term rental, sometimes for a period of months. Which method you choose to employ depends on how you feel about several things.

If you believe your business will grow rapidly, you may want to have the flexibility to move to a more powerful computer without the headache of trying to sell your own. If you believe that technology is moving so fast that any computer you purchase today will be obsolete before it has come to the end of its useful life, you may be more comfortable either renting or leasing, Finally, you may not have the cash at hand to buy a computer outright.

Leasing and rental companies are directing their marketing efforts toward businesses and established professionals, so as an individual buyer you may have problems in this area. You might be asked to leave a sizeable deposit, either in cash or as a signed credit card transaction, which the dealer will retain until you return the computer in good condition.

Computer retailers generally do not provide leasing services, but they will put you in touch with a leasing company that will buy the computer from the retailer and then lease it to you, usually for a term of several years. If you are investigating leasing, you should look into the various purchase option plans at the end of the lease term. Of course, these will vary with the lease price, but they are often tied to the fair market value of the computer at the time of lease expiration. As noted above, lessors are generally looking for business or professional lessees, or someone with an impressive credit rating.

Rentals are more suitable when you do not need a computer for an extended period of time. You may also use rentals to try out a certain hardware configuration, but this can become expensive. Rental of personal computers was not available until recently and is still not widespread.

Should you wait to acquire your computer? In its simplest form, the answer to this question revolves around economics. If the money you anticipate earning over a period of time is greater than the cost of the computer over the same period of time, then you should get the computer now. This kind of analysis, of course, is very difficult. While you can estimate your computer costs with some accuracy, your income projections could be, at worst, totally wrong. There is no real solution beyond saying that you must take risks. You can, however, minimize your risks through careful planning and a thorough analysis of your planned moonlighting activities.

How do you determine which retailer to buy your computer from? While there are no guaranteed approaches, you should look for a dealer that offers in-store courses in computers and also one that performs computer maintenance on-site. Naturally, knowledgeable sales help is a must, and personal references are a plus. If you travel with your computer you should go with a chain operation, since virtually all have some kind of reciprocal service and support agreements between franchises.

What about mail order purchases and their evident savings? Your first concern should be after-sales service, because you will not be able to establish a relationship with a retailer who may be hundreds of miles away. There is the additional risk of damage in transit. Although the experience reported by people using mail order has been very good, it may be advisable to buy your major components locally, and purchase less problematic items, such as software, by mail.

SUMMARY

The major tools and equipment needed for success as a moonlighter have to do primarily with your knowledge and experience in the field of personal computers, along with an ability to successfully market your product. Knowing how to program will be very useful, if not to write programs for sale, but to be able to understand programming techniques. Background information on personal computers should be gathered regularly from newspapers, magazines, books, and association with your peers at computer clubs and similar organizations.

Access to a personal computer is essential to gain hands-on experience and the serious moonlighter will move quickly toward the larger systems, in the £3000 to £4000 range, and up. Experience in at least one programming language is very important, as is the ability to analyze programming packages for suitability to a particular environment.

SAMPLE RESUMÉ

HARRY M. MOONLIGHTER
76 Random Road
London

Harry Moonlighter has been in the information processing industry for over ten years both as a manager of systems development for a large retailer and as a consultant. In his former capacity Harry has been heavily involved in designing and developing complex information systems and is particularly familiar with accounting and personal computers using BASIC and COBOL programming languages.

For a manufacturing company he reviewed their inventory control and reporting operations, and based on his recommendations, a personal computer was successfully installed with a purchased inventory program providing significantly improved inventory control.

Harry wrote a program to track client bookings and invoicing for a travel agency, greatly enhancing their ability to service their clients and to control their accounts better.

He has been involved in assisting many clients in introducing them to the first-time use of automated systems, and he teaches programming courses at a London college.

Educated at London University, he holds degrees in computers and business management. Harry is a member of the Data Processing Management Association and is secretary of the local IBM personal computer club.

Client references are available on request.

CHAPTER 2

FREELANCE WRITING

EQUIPMENT:
PC, typewriter

EXPERTISE:
Knowledge of at least one aspect of personal computing

CLIENT CONTACT:
Query letters, manuscript submission

FEES AND INVOICING
Per article (£45 to £80+ per 1000 words, or £150 to £300+ per article)

EXTRAS:
Word-processing; writing simple software,
reviewing hardware and software

BEGIN AT THE VERY BEGINNING

This chapter and the five that follow form the heart of *Moonlighting With Your Personal Computer*. Chapters Two to Seven outline the most promising and well-defined areas of moonlighting activity; they are arranged so that each chapter increases the level of computer ability, and the extent of contact the moonlighter has with the larger computer business world. Each reader should look through these chapters with an eye toward matching ability and knowledge of the computer to the area or areas that provide, for him or her, the most logical forum for selling their knowledge and skill. The opportunities run the range from those in this chapter, which require only a minimal contact with computing and almost no computing skill, to those set forward in Systems Houses (Chapter Seven), which require extensive knowledge of computers as used in business, along with advanced programming ability. Ambitious moonlighters will attempt to acquire the skill and savvy to enable them to move to the more demanding levels of the business, whereas the moonlighter who desires a limited, easily managed source of second income will concentrate on the less demanding areas and attempt to build a solid and stable level of activity at or close to his or her present abilities and skill. Remember that the beauty of moonlighting is its independence: you define the parameters of your work, you run your business, and you reap the rewards. The rapid deployment of personal computers in the market and in the population, and the way in which the business has evolved, give the moonlighter a rare chance to find the perfect spot within a large and varied choice of options. With this in mind, let us turn to the first of our moonlighting options, freelance writing.

WHAT IS FREELANCE WRITING?

Freelance writing is the time-honoured method used in publishing that provides readers with most of their reading matter: the author, in his own time, creates an idea or a finished work and sells it to someone who turns words into type. Except for writing that is either journalism, or tied to raising money or corporate activity (such as advertising, fund raising letters, and technical writing) nearly all published material is, to some extent, created on a freelance basis.

Writing is primarily a relationship limited to the author and his material, and publishers take advantage of this fact by tying their payments directly to what is produced. For the computer moonlighter, this situation is ideal; it means independence and freedom of choice. You may write as much, or as little, as you desire, when you want to, where you want to and you may write about anything that interests you.

The way the computer world is developing, in addition to independence, the freelance computer writer enjoys the advantage of being able to inject himself into the market at virtually any level his knowledge and skill make possible. So much money is flooding into the computer field, at all levels and in all areas, and there is so much curiosity, and such a great need for well-written and well-conceived writing about all aspects of the computer, that the freelance writer can choose from an enormous range of subject material and publishing outlets. Freelance writing, in many ways, reflects the moonlighting field as a whole: as your expertise and ability increase, you are afforded a corresponding increase in the level of your opportunity, and that upward spiral is almost unlimited. Every segment of the computer revolution carries with it a certain prerequisite of good writing, and that situation is not likely to change. Clear technical writing, imaginative descriptions of new computer applications, and new wrinkles in the computer world, as well as thorough research and the collection of information, instruction and training, and narrative accounts of the rush of computing power into a once computerless world, are all desperately needed; and people are willing to pay for these services. There will always be a need for good writing, and the field will probably never be saturated. And, keep in mind that the number of individuals with good writing skills *and* some modicum of "hard" computer knowledge is very low. If you can write well now, or are willing to put in some effort to learn, you could easily earn a healthy second income by combining that writing skill with whatever level of computer expertise you acquire.

Just to give you some idea of the breadth of this field, I've put together the following list of topics you could choose from. As you read this list, remember that this is just the tip of the iceberg, and that you will always be discovering a new topic that might be valuable to some part of your computer-using audience, and that someone, somewhere, will be willing to pay you to write about it.

- Surveys of specific aspects of personal computing, such as a class of programs or hardware.
- Reviews of new hardware products or programs.
- Actual, or possible, uses of personal computers in a particular business or industry.
- Experiences you have had with computers that pass on valuable insights to the reader.
- Relatively simple programs and games.
- Buying guides—things to consider, comparison of features.
- Humour, nostalgia, opinions, or thoughts on the general implications of the computer revolution.
- Program writing or debugging.
- Forecasts of the use of personal computer and industry trends.
- The business of personal computers.
- Documentation and instructional manuals.
- Advertising copy.

Remember, the more you learn, the more you know. If you are interested in freelance writing, you should always be considering new topics and new areas of interest. As you discover more and more about the computer, keep in mind that each step you take toward greater understanding is a step someone else has not yet taken and would probably like to read about. As you learn the ins and outs of the freelance writing world, you will begin to see how almost anything that occurs to you can be written down and sent to someone that may be interested in it.

IS IT FOR YOU?

Writing is like making love: almost everyone can do it, with one level of skill or another, and the more one does it, the better one is likely to be at it. (The connection between exceptional skill in one endeavour and exceptional skill in the other is still a matter of bitter debate in some quarters.) As one wag put it, talent is 1% inspiration and 99% perspiration. While you may not have the Great English Novel or a Pulitzer Prize-winning article lying unfinished within you, you almost certainly have the talent to create marketable freelance writing about the personal computer. The craftsmanship of good nonfiction writing requires clarity of thought, organizational skill, and the ability to edit what you write. Success in marketing one's writing is largely a matter of common sense, perseverance, and the ability to recognize patterns in the publishing world—what gets published by whom.

Practice, and a pattern of continual self-evaluation, are the largest factors in the improvement of your writing. The more you write, and the more pieces you send to publishers, the more your skill and chances for success grow. It is also a valuable practice to show your work to as many people as possible, and to collect a body of objective opinion. However, especially if you are a fledgling writer, do not take any evaluation of your work too seriously. Opinions are only opinions, and come from an infinite variety of perspectives, some more valuable than others. In terms of advice and criticism of your writing, your first rule should be: take what you need and leave the rest.

One thing to keep in mind, if you become involved with freelance writing, is that rejections, even for the most seasoned professional, almost always outweigh acceptances. If you hope for any success, you must become thick-skinned about rejection slips. Though you will become weary after receiving yet another notification that "your work does not meet our needs at the present time", you should be aware that this is often the case. Considerably less than half of all rejected articles are rejected because they are of less than marketable quality; most frequently, the article was submitted to the wrong

41

publication, or submitted at the wrong time, or carried the wrong emphasis, or a combination of all three. A rejected article can be reworked, if you find some way to improve it, but should almost always be submitted somewhere else as soon as possible. If the editor rejecting your article gives you any specific advice on improving it, you should carefully consider it. It may happen that reworking the article as suggested and resubmitting it will result in publication. If an editor gives you advice that you think is valid for all your free-lance writing, make a concerted effort to follow it. If given advice that you think is primarily applicable to that one publication, rather than to the field as a whole, keep it in mind next time you submit a manuscript or query. And, never discount the possibility that the editor is simply misinformed. If you feel that you can write an article that meets the needs of a certain publisher, do not be deterred by rejections: continue to submit articles and queries until you hit on something the editors find exactly right.

There are some habits it will pay you to cultivate as a freelance writer. Writers that make commitments to produce material in a given period of time and then miss their deadlines are very unpopular with editors and, as a result, often publish with a particular outfit only once. Take your deadlines seriously. Careful reading of poten-tial markets for your writing, with an eye toward producing exactly what their editors are looking for, can greatly increase your per-centage of acceptances. Creating an excellent article and then sending it to the wrong people, although it affirms your writing ability, is not likely to be profitable. As Nelson Bentley, the great writing instructor of the Pacific Northwest, constantly reminded his oft-published young authors, avoid self-pity like the plague. Writing is frequently a solitary, frustrating and impossible endeavour. If you have gone months with nothing but impersonal rejection slips, with the occasional exception of a snotty one, just remember to keep the faith, and realize that, in the end, "the truth will out".

Access to a word processor can make the editing of your work far less cumbersome than more primitive technologies allow. If your circumstances allow, you should seriously consider acquiring word-processing abiltiy to relieve some of the more tedious mechanical demands of freelance writing, such as retyping entire articles if you rearrange paragraphs or make a lot of typographical errors on your first draft.

Excellent articles that annoy editors because they are sloppily produced are like geode in a rock: many editors lack patience to discover the beauty within. Your manuscripts should always be typed, double spaced, on high quality paper. Follow all submission guidelines to the letter, and do not submit articles that contain typographical errors, misspellings, or a lot of corrections. Many editors reject out-of-hand any article whose physical appearance displeases them. Go out of your way to eliminate their opportunity to do so.

WHERE CAN YOU SELL YOUR WORK?

Marketing your freelance writing should be a very structured effort. You must acquire a general idea of who publishes what to decide where you should target your writing efforts. Once you have identified an area of the market that you would like to sell to, you should conduct a detailed survey of each publication, in terms of style, level of technical knowledge desired, and subjects likely to be covered. The market for computer writing is, at the moment, highly specific. Particular publishers concentrate their effort toward narrowly defined audiences. Personal computer magazines covering only one manufacturer's computer are an excellent example. If the PC you own has a magazine devoted to it, this would be one logical place to start your survey. The process is essentially the same throughout the field. If you have a particular expertise, or a particular writing skill, seek out those publishers that will best exploit your talents. If you are willing to mould your writing to fit the marketplace, select forums that provide the most opportunities within your range of skills. With sufficient patience and imagination and, in some cases, computer skill, you can probably produce saleable material for nearly all forums. Some of the principal outlets to check include the following:

MAGAZINES. Magazines about the computer, and those for the PC user, have become one of the hottest areas of magazine publishing today. An enormous number of periodicals have sprung up to serve nearly every level of computer interest and activity. A look around any newsagent's shelves or any station bookstall will show you that there are now many weekly and monthly (see Appendix C) publications devoted to personal computing as a whole or to its particular facets or particular computers, and additional magazines covering the more general computing arena. Any moonlighter with even a modicum of exposure to the world of personal computing should be able to pinpoint at least one or two magazines likely to be interested in his articles. Many general interest magazines, far removed from computer publishing, are beginning to be hungry for articles about computers written for the general public. Buy a number of magazines that look promising, read them, and send queries to those that seem to offer the best opportunity. Many magazines will provide you with a free writer's guide that can help you focus your survey further.

A partial list of PC magazines well suited to the freelance writer is provided in Appendix C to give you a start on your market survey.

TRADE JOURNALS. Trade journals are magazines devoted to a specific profession or industry. There are hundreds of these magazines, each of which provides a core of readers in nearly every human endeavour imaginable. If you have any experience with a particular business, your computer familiarity will probably allow you to write a number of articles about computer use in that field. For example, a recent article in *Theater Crafts*, a US magazine serving the technical theatre world, which outlined a proposed program to ease the set designer's chore of creating multiple perspective studies of a set's sightlines, generated considerable interest, and will most likely result in commercially available theatrical software in the near future. The section in this chapter on freelance writing as a marketing tool will suggest a valuable additional advantage offered by these trade journals.

NEWSPAPERS AND NEWSLETTERS. Newspapers all over the country are beginning to realize that interest in computers, and personal computers in particular, has generated a sizeable audience among their general readerships. Many newspapers have instituted, or are now considering, columns about the personal computer that will run on a weekly basis. If you feel that you would be able to produce a weekly article of general interest to the PC enthusiast, you might consider making your presence known to the newspapers in your area. Local newspapers and weeklies are the best candidates for the apprentice computer expert; many have not made any adjustments at all for the new popularity of computers, and may be waiting for your resumé to arrive at their offices.

ADVERTISING, DOCUMENTATION, TRAINING MANUALS AND BOOKS. For the writer with specialized writing skills or advanced computer expertise, these markets provide a wealth of opportunity. The section on advanced options, below, provides an in-depth analysis of each.

THE BUSINESS

Well-defined procedures have evolved that provide a mechanism for the selection and publication of freelance writing, and hence provide guidelines for the moonlighter hoping to get his work into print. Familiarity with the business of publishing can save you wasted effort and frustration. The following account of the traditions of publishing concentrates primarily on magazines, but may, with appropriate modification, be applied to all aspects of freelance writing.

THE WRITER'S GUIDE

Once you find a magazine that seems a likely market for your work, you should locate the address in the front of the publication and write to request a writer's guide. Although not all magazines have pre-pared writing guides, some of the most promising candidates for the moonlighter do have such guides. What you should receive is a brief summary of the audience the magazine is intended to serve, an out-line of the type of articles the editors are looking for, and the physical specifications for manuscripts that are submitted. Although the guidelines for content will vary from magazine to magazine, the pre-ferred form of manuscript is essentially the same.

• Type the article, double spaced, on good quality A4 paper with wide margins.

• Any illustrations must be supplied with captions.

• Photographs should be sharp and, if necessary, in colour.

• Program listings, if included, are often photographed rather than typeset, so they should be typed with a new ribbon and be letter perfect.

Requests for writer's guides should always include a self-addressed, stamped envelope (SAE). In general, publishers will not respond to requests or return submissions if you do not include postage and a self-addressed envelope.

THE QUERY LETTER

If the writer's guide or answering letter reinforces your interest in a particular publication, you should think of an idea for an article that fits its needs and send in a query (also called a *proposal*). Your query should be single spaced on A4 paper. The first two or three paragraphs should provide a readable, condensed account of your proposed article. This summary should be detailed, but it *must* be brief. The rest of your letter should include your qualifications including, if possible, any previous published articles, the readers likely to be interested in your article, an estimate of its length (in words, not pages), how soon your manuscript can be delivered, and should mention any illustrations or program listings you intend to include.

THE ARTICLE

In some cases, an editor will express an interest in your proposal, but will ask you to alter it in some way. If the suggestions are acceptable to you, rewrite and resubmit your proposal as quickly as possible. If the editor likes your proposal enough to ask for the article, then you are in business. Write your article, using the writer's guide and your proposal as an outline, and send it in. Some magazines will ask you, especially if you are new to freelance writing, to submit your article on spec, which means that the editor is interested in seeing your article, but will evaluate your article according to specifications before publishing it or forwarding you any money. If an accepted proposal leads to the production of a rejected manuscript, you should, if possible, rewrite the article and submit it again. An editor will generally give you some reason for rejecting an article he or she has asked to see. If this is not possible, or still does not result in publication, send a query elsewhere, indicating that the article is already written, though without mentioning that it has been rejected elsewhere. Many experienced freelancers have a policy of doing work on spec, and some freelancer's associations are quite intolerant of the practice. You should do work on spec only at the beginning of your moonlighting career. Once you have established some sort of track record, you should try to get a "kill fee" agreement. A kill fee, usually provided when the proposed article is of substantial length, is an agreement from the publisher that they will pay you a set fee, generally 10% to 20% of the purchase price of the article, even if it is not used, in return for the time and effort you spend producing a piece to the editor's specifications. The availability of a kill fee will vary from publisher to publisher, but it is insurance that you will not work for nothing, it is valuable and you should make an effort to find publishers who will offer it to you.

PAYMENT

The payments available to the magazine writer will usually be outlined in the writer's guide. They range from £50 to £70 per page of typeset material. An examination of the magazine should enable you to figure the payment per word, or per page of typescript. Some magazines will pay a flat fee in the £150 to £300 range, and some will pay by the word, though this is rare and a rate would need to be negotiated specifically. Writer's guides will give you the minimum and maximum length accepted. Though some magazines pay on acceptance, many do not pay their authors until the article is actually published. Turnaround time varies immensely, but delays of three months after acceptance are not uncommon. Keep this in mind when budgeting your profits from freelance writing.

ADVANCED OPTIONS

Though a freelance writing moonlighter can happily limit the market to magazines, there are other publishing opportunities available to particularly ambitious or talented individuals. These writing outlets are generally more demanding, and some carry considerably more risk than magazine writing in terms of time spent unprofitably or financial investment placed at risk, but the potential payoffs are proportionately greater.

BOOKS

If you have a unique angle on the computer, or a wealth of experience in a particular area, you may be able to put together a more sustained and involved writing project: an entire book. There is now a flood of books on the market that cover a wide variety of personal computing topics. Some of the most successful provide how-to instruction on some particular task, such as programming in a particular language or for a particular application; using a specific piece of software or a specific hardware system; using the PC to get rich, as an educational tool, or in business; buying (or designing) a computer system; and, literally, hundreds of other topics. Many books with the potential for a substantial audience are yet to be written. A book represents a great investment of time and energy, and you should evaluate realistically the time you will need and the level of your expertise before agreeing to produce one. But, if you think you have enough insights to fill an entire book on a particular topic, by all means investigate the possibility of getting one to press. *The Writers' & Artists' Yearbook* (published annually) can help you determine the interests of hundreds of publishers, and advertisements in computer magazines can lead you to other likely prospects. Look also at the special twice-yearly "export" edition of *The Bookseller,* to be fully aware of publishers current lists.

As with magazine articles, do not send an unsolicited manuscript; compose a proposal that includes a summary and a table of contents, as well as a writing sample that has been published, if possible. You might also include a rough estimate of the size of the potential market based on similar books, if the figures are available to you. Limit your proposal to two pages.

Payments for books vary as much as for magazine articles, if not more. If you get a percentage of sales (a *royalty*) it will probably be approximately 7% to 10% of the retail price or of the publishers' receipts. If you are to receive royalties, you should try to obtain an advance. If you are paid a flat fee, particularly common in the trade-paperback market, you should estimate the number of hours you are likely to spend researching and writing the book, and negotiate payment for at least £30 per thousand words. Nearly all book publishing is based on a contractual agreement between the publisher and author. If such an agreement is not offered by your prospective publisher, seriously consider looking elsewhere. Should the publisher draw up a contract for your approval, examine it carefully, and consider retaining an agent or, at the least, consulting a published author, to check the contract out for you. If a publisher goes to the trouble of sending you a contract, he is very interested in your book, and you should discuss with him any clause of which you are unsure.

SELF-PUBLISHING

Publishers give authors only a small percentage of their revenues because they are responsible for editing costs, production costs, distribution and marketing. They also provide the author with the advantage of a proven reputation alongside other well-known authors. However, the moonlighter can bypass this middleman by self-publishing, taking all the risks, and enjoying all the profits. You should limit yourself in the beginning to small pamphlets, which are inexpensively reproduced and advertised, and cover a very specific topic. Such a pamphlet can be advertised in computer periodicals with national circulation for about £70 for an eighth page per issue for classified advertising. Reproduction and mailing can run as low as £1 per copy. Depending on length, content and what you think the market will bear, you may charge £3.50 to £7.00 per copy. Advertising a successful pamphlet in multiple issues of the same magazine can further enhance your profit margin.

A pamphlet directed toward corporate executives, covering a broad managerial computer issue, outlining the impact of PCs on a particular industry, or identifying trends that might give your reader a jump on his competition, can be even more profitable. To reach this market, you should use direct mail. Produce a description of your pamphlet and compile a mailing list of executives likely to be interested in your topic. Though there are companies that specialize in supplying mailing lists, the moonlighter working on a shoestring can compile an effective list through research in the library. Trade directories and specialist year books are excellent aids for compiling mailing lists. Because your expertise is greater than the author of the more general pamphlet, and because your marketing costs are higher and your material is purchased using corporate, rather than in-dividual, money you should charge accordingly for each copy, somewhere in the £10 to £25+ range.

A mail order response of 10% is considered excellent, and 5% very good. You should control costs and prepare your list so that 2% sales will be your break-even point. If your report attracts a good response, you could make a profit of £600, or more.

In both types of self-publication, you should include a note with each pamphlet sold thanking the purchaser for his business, and asking for any comments that may help you improve your product, or suggestions for other topics for which there may be a demand.

ADVERTISING

Though writing for the purpose of advertising is a special skill (unlike all other writing), good "copy" commands a premium in any market. This is true particularly in the computer market, where competition is fierce, and the products are relatively new and constantly updated. The largest hardware and software manu-facturers, of course, employ high-power professional advertising agencies, but there are hundreds of small computer concerns in the market, supplying everything from hardware and peripherals to disks to computer "supplies" like disk storage, paper, and printing ribbons. As in publishing, the computer revolution has caused a lot

49

of stir in the advertising world. There is absolutely no standard way of entering this field. Look for advertising in as many places as possible, starting with computer magazines, catalogues and the newspapers. Look for products that you are familiar with, or ones with particularly wretched ads. If you have any professional experience in advertising or marketing, you should be able to make a good case to the company involved of the value of your services. If you are new to the field, you might consider rewriting a particularly bad advertisement, sending it to the company and offering your services. A less pointed method involves submitting ads of a more general nature, for instance, for a fictional company, as a sample of the kind of advertising work of which you are capable. Freelance copywriters generally receive about £20 to £25 per hour, so you might begin negotiations with this figure. Expect a wide range of payment, though, and always be prepared to supply a bid on a per-piece basis.

DOCUMENTATION

Documentation for personal computer software has a reputation that ranges from good to very poor, with most clustered at the low end of the spectrum. Program authors are often extremely good at writing code, but their intimate acquaintance with their program's most technical details, as well as an occasional horrible set of English writing skills, leads them to supply nearly unusable instructions to the end user of their work. One of the largest gaps in the computer world is the near absence of people who can understand some of the more esoteric and complicted computer territories and write well, particularly if clear and understandable technical writing is required. If you have a background in technical writing, or even have a good prose style, your most promising area may well be the writing of documentation.

If you can place yourself in the position of a reader who has no experience with the program at hand, and can produce documentation that answers the reader's questions and caters to his or her needs, there are two pursuits that merit your attention: initial documentation and secondary documentation.

INITIAL DOCUMENTATION. You should approach the programmer directly, or the publisher of a program, and offer your writing services as part of the marketing preparation of the program. At the moment, there is no traditional mechanism for marketing this skill. Computer clubs and computer periodicals probably provide the best way to reach the individual programmer before he submits his program to a distributor. If you would like to establish some kind of continuing relationship with a particular publisher, my only advice is that you contact the company directly. Write a letter outlining your skills, both in writing and in computer use, and suggest that a meeting would work to the mutual advantage of both parties. As far as fees go, you are on your own. This opportunity is virgin territory, and hardly any figures have surfaced. However, many fulltime freelance documentation writers report sizeable earnings each year providing this one specialized skill to those who need it.

SECONDARY DOCUMENTATION. The second possibility to explore is producing documentation, usually in book form, which replaces less-than-perfect documentation provided with the software. This sort of documentation is also an excellent candidate for the self-publishing scenario sketched earlier. When looking for an opening to begin writing secondary documentation, you should concentrate on finding a popular piece of software with unsatisfactory documentation that has not been covered by another freelancer already. Your own PC experience, and detailed conversations with heavy PC users should provide you with the most solid information in evaluating your choice. Once you identify your target, gain access to the program and its documentation. Use the software, evaluate the documentation, and form a general idea of what improvements you might make. You should then write a proposal outlining the shortcomings of the original documentation and your suggestions for its improvement, along with the rest of the background covered in the section on "The Query Letter." Your proposal should be posted in the following order: 1) the original publisher of the program, 2) book publishers specializing in the computer trade, and 3) general interest publishers, starting with those most technically inclined. The documentation you actually write should include clear examples of the program as it is used, and a trouble-shooting guide that corrects the problems you had when running the program. Payment usually will follow the schedule outlined in the section on book publishing, but if you think you have found a large source of user frustration, you should try to negotiate a percentage of the revenue, rather than accept a flat fee, to cash in on the popularity of your documentation.

FREELANCE WRITING AS A MARKETING TOOL

In the chapters that follow, you will sometimes run across the suggestion that you use freelance writing forums as a part of your marketing plan. In general, this involves providing information about your product or service that is geared toward the general reader or a particular audience likely to be interested in your work. This may simply make your name and work known to those who might provide you with profitable employment in the future, or may result in specific inquiries being directed to you. This marketing tool is directly applicable to magazine publishing. Though some publications may have questions about the propriety of publishing such a "puff piece" (you are puffing yourself up, giving yourself a plug), many are just as likely to see it as a valuable piece of news concerning the activities of their readers, and as a service to those who desire to be aware of the most current developments. This kind of writing is mainly useful to the PC moonlighter who provides a specific, potentially popular product to a well-defined market. A consultant or contract programmer who concentrates in one particular industry is a prime example. Though computer magazines are a valuable forum, a trade journal serving the computer industry is more likely to provide the kind of readership that makes such a piece a valuable marketing tool. Readers of trade journals are usually bright executives in decision-making positions, frequently in companies that are at the forefront of their industries, or those that are not as well known, but willing to conside any reasonable method that might improve their position within the industry. Trade journals, more than other types of periodicals, have as one of their principal aims the provision of forward-thinking news on state-of-the-art business practices, as well as reports of the next important breakthrough, in their readers' fields. A moonlighter involved in an enterprise likely to be served by such freelance writing might give himself an enormous competitive edge by writing and placing accounts of his new and important work in a publication highly visible to many of his potential clients.

THE FUTURE

The need for writing about every aspect of the computer field will not only dramatically increase with the growth of personal computer use in general, but will possibly grow with even more vigour than the computer market as a whole. Publishers enthusiastically jump on the bandwagon of a new wrinkle in the habits and lives of their readers. While the recent explosion of words about computers may be diminished in the next few years, chances are just as good that the market, especially for magazines, will continue to grow as publishers and editors discover new audiences or new ways to package their wares. The more advanced options outlined in this chapter are not likely to decrease as long as there is a market for computers; and computers seem to be here to stay. A quick-witted, flexible moonlighter could pursue his or her first entry into the writing market down innumerable paths, leading to opportunities greater than they could have hoped. In the "Information Age", knowledge sells: not only will people pay for your knowledge, but what you learn in writing about computers may well place you in a position of enormous power in the computer world.

SAMPLE QUERY LETTER

December 1, 1984

Mr David Jones, Editor
XYZ Computer Magazine
Horton Street
London

Dear Mr Jones:

I am interested in writing an article about hard disks for personal computers that reviews their place in the personal computer field today and forecasts their role in the future. The decreasing costs for hard disks are making them more attractive but there are certain things the prospective user should watch out for that will be discussed in my article.

Initially I describe the features of hard disks and compare their operation with soft or floppy disks. I then analyze hard and soft (floppy) disks as to their cost effectiveness and talk about the impact of hard disks on copy-protected software. Covered in this article will be programs that allow you to copy software easily onto hard disks and the trends in the availability of hard disks with software already on them. The increasing number of software packages requiring hard disks will also be discussed. Particular attention will be paid to the problems hard disk users encounter with back-ups and the various options to solve this problem.

I estimate that this article will be about 4000 words, and I can provide several sketches of the features of a hard disk. The basis for some of the research for this article is a broad collection of marketing material and discussions with several hard disk users, members of my personal computer club. I am a hard disk user myself and have made a serious study of the products before making my purchase.

I estimate I could have the article ready in about four weeks after your go ahead.

Enclosed is a stamped, self-addressed envelope for your reply.

Sincerely,

David Q. Writer
76 Random Road
London
Telephone: 01-666-3434

■■■■■■■■■■■■■■■■■■■■
■■■■■■■■■■ CHAPTER 3 ■ ■ ■ ■ ■ ■ ■ ■

SERVICE BUREAUX

EQUIPMENT:
PC, specialized software, printer

EXPERTISE:
At least one specialized software application

CLIENT CONTACT:
Assignment and delivery of projects, either one-time or on a
continuing basis

FEES AND INVOICING:
Per job, or monthly for continuing services

EXTRAS:
Word-processing, letter-quality printer

WHAT IS A SERVICE BUREAU?

Of all the opportunities outlined in this book, the service bureau
offers the personal computer user the richest option and the most
easily entered field of moonlighting. The service bureau offers a wide
variety of computer applications to anyone who desires the advantages of the computer but is not willing or able to acquire one.
Purchasing and learning to use even one specialized piece of software
can enable a PC user to turn the home into a business. The number of
individuals and small businesses who only occasionally require
computer processing, or whose limited computer needs do not, at
that moment, justify the purchase of an entire PC system, is very
large. If you are new to computing or do not want to commit a lot of
time to your moonlighting venture, providing services to these
people could well be the most logical way to start recouping your
computer investments.

The concept of the commercial service bureau was developed
when computers were so expensive that even large businesses could

not afford them. When computers were relatively scarce, the competitive edge of computer processing could often be obtained only by delivering data to someone with a computer, and waiting for the output, which was rather expensive. With the introduction of the PC, an entire new level of service-bureau functions was opened up. Now, it is fairly easy for an individual to form an independent service bureau, serving customers who were previously priced out of reach of the computer revolution. As a moonlighter providing computer services, you will receive input from your customer (input that can range from a mailing list, to an exam project, to weekly payroll information), process the data, and deliver the output. The number of data-processing services you might provide is enormous, limited only by the software available and your imagination. Moonlighters who have some programming ability can even write their own applications packages to provide services not available from off-the-shelf software. Some of the more lucrative services are summarized in the following six sections.

WORD-PROCESSING

Word-processing requires a somewhat larger capital investment, but it is one of the most popular computer services. There is a large number of people out there who would pay for word-processing, but who will not buy a PC and do it themselves. College students often do not have the patience, typing skill, or time to produce letter-perfect versions of their written work. Job hunters need to have resumés that can be updated and altered to fit the particular job they are seeking at a given time. Professional writers working deadlines are natural consumers for a freelance word-processor's services, as are political parties that need a backlog of speeches that can be readily changed to reflect constantly shifting political positions. Anyone who works with words, especially words that require some level of continuous editing, will be tempted by the advantages of this type of service bureau.

To run a word-processing service, you will need to purchase a word-processing program and a printer. There are more than fifty word-processing packages currently available on the market, so shopping for the best combination of price and performance is strongly advised. Printers can be expensive. Remember that if you get a dot-matrix printer, which is less expensive, you will appeal to a limited market simply because the quality of the print is too low for most applications. A letter-quality printer should be considered a necessity, and the cost runs from £350 to £2000.

ACCOUNTING AND TAX PREPARATION

The most popular accounting service you might provide on a continuing basis is the preparation of weekly payrolls. There is packaged software available to run this application, so you will not have to write your own program. If you are running a customer's payroll, you will receive data from him for each pay period, process the information, and print the pay slips for him. In addition, you will have to maintain a master file of employee information and up-to-date figures. A certain amount of familiarity with basic accounting is, of course, a considerable advantage to the moonlighter interested in providing this service. Accuracy and attention to deadlines are very important here.

Tax preparation, though more seasonal, is an excellent area for the moonlighter to consider. However, keep in mind that the service you provide is no substitute for professional tax counselling, and you should make this clear to your customers. There are several tax packages available in the off-the-shelf software market. The range of prices, from several hundred to several thousand pounds, encompasses a broad array of capabilities. The most powerful of these systems can handle 20 to 30 forms, transfer numbers from form to form, easily calculate the advantages of different tax strategies, and even prepare your tax returns. Another class of tax program is the tax template, which is used in conjunction with a spread-sheet program such as VisiCalc or SuperCalc. These programs are particularly good for comparing different ways to prepare complex returns (playing the "what if" game) and some have special features; for instance, flagging for further consideration itemized deductions that exceed statistical limits. The primary advantage of these templates is that, if you already own the primary program that drives them, they are very inexpensive and very powerful.

PROPERTY MANAGEMENT

Providing computerized record keeping for property managers is another possibility for your service bureau. Several programs are available, usually in the £200 to £500 range, which provide book-keeping functions, as well as tracking data such as the availability of apartments, late payment reminders, and printing cheques. *The*

Landlord, by Systems Plus, Inc., and *The Apartment House Manager*, by User Friendly Software are examples of currently available US property-management programs.

MAILING LISTS

Many organizations need to keep lists of names and addresses that must be updated and printed frequently. Artists, businesses, churches, community groups and political organizations often maintain mailing lists and are very likely to consider a well-run service to take over their clerical work. Because the computer expertise required is minimal and once the list is on file, the moonlighter will be involved only with occasional updating and print-outs, this kind of service can be the ideal first step for the fledgling service bureau. A printer will be necessary, of course, and you will have to either buy or write a program. Cross-referencing your list by age, income, location and similar defining characteristics is an excellent selling point.

EDUCATION

One of the most promising areas for the moonlighting computer user involves providing training of some kind. Classes on PC use in general, word-processing and other specialized applications, and specific computer languages have all proved very successful for moonlighters. You may provide instruction in your home, at your students' homes or, if you are more qualified, at an adult education centre, local college, or computer store. Computer knowledge is at a premium at the moment; and personal instruction will be sought for quite some time to come.

RENTAL

You may also consider renting time on your computer. If you have specialized software, such as word-processing, your system is more likely to be attractive to a number of people than is an "unadorned" PC. But even without special software, there will be people who would like to try out a computer before they buy one, or might like to use your computer to produce their own software. Charging between £5 and £10 an hour is more or less standard for providing this service. You should also consider working out an agreement with another moonlighter to provide back-up computers to each other in the event of a breakdown.

The six areas I have mentioned are just the tip of the iceberg. Once you have had some experience with the computer and have a feel for what other people find PCs useful for, you will undoubtedly develop some ideas of your own. Service bureaux can be designed to fit your equipment and your personal tastes and skills; you should consider offering any service for which you feel there is a market.

IS IT FOR YOU?

What are the skills and personality traits that can best help you meet the challenges of running a service bureau? Though the diversity of the work makes general rules difficult to devise, I have identified and expanded on some things that I think might prove to be helpful.

COMPUTER ABILITIES

Although you can operate a service bureau without a high level of computer expertise, especially if you plan to use packaged software, there are some minimum requirements. You must be familiar enough with your computer and its operation to track down easily and correct any trouble you run into, and to avoid some of the more basic operator errors. And you do need an in-depth understanding of the application you are going to run; you should be familiar with the program you are using, and have enough background to choose an off-the-shelf program that best suits your needs. If you want to make alterations to your purchased software package, you will need some programming ability in the language in which the program is written. However, except for freelance writing no moonlighting area in this book has less rigid requirements for computer abilities than the service bureau. Remember that, at the most basic level, you are selling operational expertise, and you will occasionally have to correct minor hardware and software problems without jeopardizing your deadlines, so you should have a solid knowledge of the ins and outs of your system before you start your business.

ORGANIZATION

All jobs that your service bureau takes on will carry a deadline with them. Reliability is one of the strongest selling points you have, especially for any continuing assignment you undertake. Deadline pressures are a normal part of the service-bureau business, so, to ensure smooth operation, you should be capable of organizing and coordinating many separate activities. Remember too, that you should always allow enough time to cope with unexpected problems and bad data. Access to another computer is vital so that, if the worst comes to the worst and you cannot use your system, you will still be able to deliver output on time. A back-up computer can be arranged through a friend or a computer club, and usually involves a reciprocal arrangement of some kind. Since most of the work is done in your own time, there should be little difficulty in scheduling this type of moonlighting around your 9-to-5 job. Remember, accurate estimates of your turn-around time for a particular job are the only way you can ensure that you will be able to deliver work on time.

ACCURACY

If you are handling any sort of accounting data, it is absolutely essential that every piece of data in your system is accurate. Your reputation depends on complete accuracy every time. Even the service-bureau activities that do not directly involve your customers' finances demand a high degree of accuracy. If you are careful, and are very attentive to detail, you are naturally suited to provide this kind of service.

RUNNING THE BUSINESS

Running a service bureau requires very little direct contact with your clients. Your meetings with them will be limited to pickups and deliveries in almost all cases. If you do not hold business relations to be your strongest suit, you will probably be happy with the more or less solitary nature of running a service bureau.

WHO HIRES SERVICE BUREAUX?

The service bureau provides a low-cost way for individuals and businesses to acquire limited applications of computing power. This is the only moonlighting area in which you will find a large percentage of the market to be individuals. While payroll preparation and similar applications are geared towards the small businessman or accounting firms many, like tax preparation and word-processing, draw their largest share of customers from private individuals. In general, service-bureau customers are likely to be those with an occasional or limited need for computer-processing capabilities, but who are not in a position to provide a computer themselves. In the section on marketing below, I will give you some hints on how to make your service bureau known to those who may be interested.

YOU AND YOUR CUSTOMER

As mentioned earlier, your contact with your customer is likely to be limited. For the most part, he will deliver, or post, the input to you and you will get the output back to him at some specified time. For work that takes place on a regular, continuing basis, your client contact will be more extensive, and your fee should reflect this. Again, the two most important things to keep in mind for customer satisfaction are accuracy and reliability. Because much of your new business will come from recommendations, a reputation for delivering error-free work on time should form the core of your customer-relations effort.

CONTRACTS AND WARRANTIES

A large proportion of service-bureau business is conducted on a relatively informal basis. For the more complex services, though, you may want to consider developing a written agreement modelled on the following guidelines—while remembering that they are guidelines only which are subject to overall legal requirements:

- An introduction that explains in general terms the work to be done and states the names of the parties involved.
- A section that describes in some detail the inputs to the system (usually provided by the customer), including their format and frequency, and the processing you agree to provide, also defined in terms of format and frequency. You may also incorporate in this clause any documentation that describes your program's operation in detail.
- The time you are allowed for processing the customer's data per the specifications on which you agreed.
- Your fee schedule and payment terms.
- A statement of limited warranty that limits your liability to performance in accordance with the specifications set forth in item 2 above.
- A statement that you will hold information concerning your customer's business in strictest confidence.
- A summary of your back-up procedures and, if agreed to, an arrangement to store a copy of your master file on your customer's premises.

FEES

Naturally, the fees you charge will vary greatly depending on the type of work you do. There are no standard hourly fees for this sort of work, so you will have to develop your own fee structure. For many applications, you will probably want to devise fees keyed to the number of transactions, according to job, page, change or some other criteria. Your fees should take into account the following factors.

- Your time
- The cost of your computer
- The cost of your software

This sort of analysis will yield only a rough figure, and you should take into consideration the competition's prices. Following are the typical figures you might use in arriving at your fee:

- Your time: £10 to £20 per hour
- Personal computer time at a rate that assumes recouping a £5000 system investment in two years at 4 hours per day and 100 days per year
- Software: 75p per hour or less

Some typical per item charges are

Mailing list: 50p for each added name, 10p for each label printed

Word-processing: 75p to £1.30 per page

MARKETING

The process of developing a marketing plan should begin with the consideration of the nature of your enterprise. You are selling the capabilities of your system and your own expertise. One of your strongest selling points is that computer work can be done more efficiently by someone who has your experience in the field and can spread overhead costs among all his customers. The many varieties of services you might offer call for a variety of marketing techniques. For instance, income tax preparation is a somewhat seasonal enterprise. Word-processing services can be advertised on notice boards and in college magazines; and you might also approach large word-processing firms with an offer to cover their occasional overflow work. Do not neglect such humble advertising venues as post-office boards and leaflets. You may be surprised at the number of people in your area or even in your street, interested in word-processing, a resumé service or mailing-list maintenance. The convenience of running a business close to your home can contribute a great deal towards increasing the pleasure of your moonlighting work.

General advertising venues include newspapers, computer magazines and ads on your local radio. Stress the convenience and accuracy of computers, and do not hesitate to play up the remaining mystique of the computer in your ads. You might also consider direct mail as a source for new business. If your service is more or less confined to one business, you could go through the phone book for a list of names and addresses, or investigate companies that sell mailing lists. Small accounting firms are good candidates for some service bureaux, as are travel agencies and estate agents.

I recommend that, at least in the beginning, you confine your marketing efforts to your immediate geographic area. Running a service bureau provides enough challenges without adding the logistical headaches of the post or other delivery systems. Besides, most users appreciate the personal attention of an occasional visit from their computer expert!

SPECIAL PROBLEMS AND OPPORTUNITIES

You may encounter some strong competition in trying to establish your new service bureau, especially if you are attempting to provide some of the more high-powered applications outlined here, such as tax preparation or payroll service. There are established, fulltime service bureaux out there, and in some cases there are specialists who will be in direct competition with you. If you can offer a service at lower cost, or quicker delivery than your competition, you can maintain a competitive edge, even against established professionals. You may also encounter customers who are dubious about the part-time nature of your business. Again, low costs are one of the best arguments to allay such doubts, and you may also want to offer a special introductory offer, such as providing processing at very low cost or even gratis, for a limited period, to demonstrate your professionalism and reliability.

Equipment breakdowns and software bugs may occasionally threaten your deadlines. In addition to the back-up systems suggested earlier, you can minimize this potential problem by using a well-seasoned software system. When you buy a software package, one of your prime considerations must be reliability, best insured by market testing. If a program has been on the market for approximately one year, the chances are good that most of the bugs have been removed. Also reliable hardware maintenance, whether provided by your retailer, the manufacturer or a third party, is very important.

Especially in business-oriented services, data security and integrity can be a problem. If you are doing any sort of work that requires you to keep a running master file of any kind, a year-to-date payroll system, for example, it is vitally important that you keep a back-up copy, which is always up to date, in a separate, preferably fire-resistant, location. One of the best solutions to this problem is to get your customer to agree to keep a copy of your master-job file at his office. If there is ever a fire, flood or other disaster that involves your computer system, the last thing you will want to worry about is your customer data. For the same reason, you should make a general practice of storing secure copies of all your software.

Data integrity is a completely different problem. Some customers' input, particularly in the beginning, is occasionally unreadable or incorrect. As your customer becomes more familiar with your operation, such data rejects should taper off. You should make sure, however, that all your software has some sort of method of identifying bad data. Some software packages include a strict edit subroutine; if you write your own program, be sure to include this feature. You must always have some sort of operational mechanism that will alert you to careless mistakes before they cause delays, or worse, begin to spread throughout your database and master files. An error that is caught too late can sometimes be impossible to get back out of your system.

A final problem that is peculiar to the service bureau can often be turned into a golden opportunity. At some time, your client may inform you that he has decided to acquire his own computer system, and will no longer be needing your services. It is inevitable that some of your customers will have used your service bureau as a stop-gap until they were ready to join the computer revolution themselves. When this point is reached, you should make every effort to offer your services as a consultant (see Chapter Six for the ins and outs of consulting). Because you have been providing your customer with all the computing power he has needed up to this point, and because you are obviously a professional in his eyes, who could be better suited to ease his transition into the computer age than you? It is possible that when you reach this point, you may find yourself prepared to move into more complicated areas of moonlighting.

THE FUTURE

With the decreasing cost of PCs, and the increasing operational ease, capacity and variety of software packages, the growth of major service bureaux has slowed somewhat, but they still remain a thriving segment of the computer industry. Set against this trend, though, is the increasingly widespread acceptance and popularity of the PC, which provides a steadily increasing market from which to draw customers. There will always be those who want the advantages of computers, but cannot be bothered with the expense and effort of acquiring their own and learning to use them: that is where *you* enter the picture.

■■■■■■■■■■■■■■■■■■
■■■■■■■■■CHAPTER 4■■■■■■■■■

PACKAGED PROGRAMS

EQUIPMENT:
PC, Printer

EXPERTISE:
Advanced programming ability

CLIENT CONTACT:
Contact with distributors; possible modification and upkeep of
programs

FEES AND INVOICING
With a distributor: 5% to 20% royalty from gross receipts
Self-marketing: profit per software unit sold

EXTRAS:
Graphics package, colour terminal

The personal computer cannot operate without software, just as a
record player is useless without albums to play. Just as young
musicians do not manufacture stereos, you will not design hardware
in your spare time. But software is another matter. Countless chores
and diversions can be accomplished with a PC once the software is
available, and the creation of software provides an enormous opportunity for the moonlighter.

Of the six moonlighting areas I discuss in this book, software
packaging is, without doubt, the fastest growing. personal computer
sales are running like wildfire through many segments of the
economy and through thousands of homes. Every hardware system
sold guarantees an average software sale of about £500. Hundreds of
thousands of pounds are being spent on software, and moonlighting
programmers are in a perfect position to lay claim to some of this
fortune.

MARKET SURVEY

The revenue generated by the PC software market in 1983 was well over the projections. Sales are projected to expand to enormous proportions in the next five years. But don't let the enormity of these sales figures lead you to believe that you cannot find a place in the market; the field is far from being closed. In fact, writing software represents a classic opportunity. The introduction of new technology always opens the door to those of us who are quick witted and talented enough to move in and establish a presence. And the timing for PC software is perfect right now. The market is booming, and the moonlighter, who is rewarded not with a salary, not with fringe benefits, but with a share of the revenue his work generates, is the logical market actor to provide the products demanded by the consumer. The analogy made earlier to the music business provides valuable insight for the part-time programmer. Programming, like musicianship, is "labour intensive": the raw materials are creativity, imagination and talent; the capital investment is relatively minor. Record producers have long relied on individual, unrewarded effort to supply their industry with talented, primarily self-educated young performers hungry for success. In both music and programming it is not until a marketable product is actually produced that its creator enters the marketplace. Thus, only those portions of the industry beyond the means of the individual—efficient mass production, advertising, packaging, large-scale distribution and retail sales on a national level—are left to fulltime professionals. Large numbers of programs currently available were created by independent programmers, often working part-time.

Fortunes have been made by software authors, some writing business software, some creating games and some writing for the home market. Estimates of the number of software packages range from 5000 to more than 20,000. The application areas served by this flood of software include:

- Accounting (probably the largest)
- Games
- Word processing
- Payroll and personnel
- Education
- Government
- Manufacturing

- Sales
- Law
- Banking
- Insurance

The prices of these packages range from £20 to over £3000. At this point, nearly all software is targeted for the office or the home. Though there is some overlap, the novice software author should consider directing his or her efforts toward a specific segment of the market, as taste and judgment dictate. Business software is focused primarily on money and data management: countless accounting applications, multivariable spread-sheets, inventory control and file management, which includes personnel records, mailing lists, and memo networks, make up the bulk of this market. Programs targeted for home use include games, educational software aimed at both children and adults, and home budget aids. Word-processing provides one of the few areas of significant overlap. Moonlighters should not be too wary of the separation between home and office, but should be aware that writing programs for one or the other can greatly simplify marketing problems.

CASE HISTORIES

The examples included in this section are drawn from the lives of successful entrepreneurs in the field of packaged software. While these scenarios were played out within a frame of fulltime operations, each of the paths explored could have been travelled on a moonlighting basis, although not as quickly.

One. The first entrepreneur was a PC user who bought a word-processing package from a major hardware vendor; the package was so bad he decided that he could easily write a better one. He had some experience in computer programming and already knew several programming languages, and that background proved to be a considerable advantage. Selecting a low-level language (i.e. less English-like, more efficient because of its similarity to machine language) he had a workable model in three weeks. After three months of intensive testing and debugging, he rented a booth at a local computer fair and placed a small advertisement in a computer magazine. In about one and a half years, his program was widely accepted and has since sold over 25,000 copies. The ongoing success of the programmer's product is due in no small measure to the excellent customer support he offers, and to an accessible hot-line.

Two. Another software author began by frequenting a local computer retail store and getting jobs consulting for customers who were having problems with their PCs. He then went to work for a successful PC software house. From there, he assembled a team consisting of himself, another programmer whose software knowledge was superior to his, and a venture capitalist. This team developed and marketed one of the most successful multifunction—database, graphics, and spread-sheet—packages today. An important ingredient of their success was the thorough testing prior to release, which made the package "bullet proof", that is, virtually impossible to crash through operator errors. In the first nine months, 50,000 copies of his program were sold.

Three. An executive of a company in the clothing industry lost his job when his company was acquired by a larger firm. He purchased an Apple computer and VisiCalc and became a consultant, knowing little more than how to turn on the computer. In a year, he had developed a substantial business selling computer-modelling software for business, including a program that analyzes branch-store operations budgets versus actual performance. In addition to this type of work, he has begun teaching this technique, and writing a VisiCalc column for a local computer newsletter.

PERSONAL CHARACTERISTICS NEEDED FOR PACKAGING PROGRAMS
PERSONALITY

Some of the areas of moonlighting discussed in this book could be attempted by almost anyone. Although the opportunities of programming are many, the personality traits necessary to attempt it successfully are rather specific. The single most important characteristic is patience. Programming can be very frustrating, since the computer cannot adjust itself for human imperfection; it cannot decide what you meant, only what you said. Every keystroke means something: a single misplaced comma, typographical error or extra space can render an entire program unworkable, or provide slighly skewed results in very special cases. If producing lengthy, complicated projects that must be letter perfect strains your patience, you may not find programming to your liking. On the other hand, if you are a perfectionist, a tinkerer, have a vast supply of patience and like to do detailed work, this might be your cup of tea. If you are to create a working program that is competitive, you must be prepared to go through the code many times, make endless minor adjustments, run it again and again, and occasionally stare at the unforgiving screen without a clue as to what to try next.

Programming is a solitary endeavour—only rarely can the task be subdivided by members of a team—a relationship between the programmer and his program. You will need concentration, and aptitude for detail, and the willingness to work long hours to meet contractual deadlines. Writing programs involves thinking clearly, breaking a large job into the smallest meaningful pieces, organizing and pruning a solution down to its barest essentials; at its best, it involves imagination, cleverness and what engineers call elegance. It is especially well suited to those people who truly enjoy solving problems that require the vigorous application of logic.

KNOWLEDGE

Naturally, the moonlighter with a chance of success in software packaging must be a very competent programmer, if not an expert. Power in a PC, measured both by CPU speed and memory space, creates an absolute theoretical limit to the capabilities of applications programs; thus, in-depth knowledge of, and facility with, an efficient programming language such as assembler or C Language is absolutely essential. Compiler BASIC is, in special cases, an additional possibility. Briefly, computer languages are characterized against a scale that runs from *efficient, low-level*, the lowest being machine language (the strings of ones and zeroes the CPU actually receives from the operating system after your disk has been read), to *high-level* languages, which are high in the sense of approaching English. A high-level language, such as BASIC, is easier for the beginner to learn and use because it is not as foreign to the way humans talk and think as are the low-level languages—but, because it is skewed toward programmer convenience, it is harder for the computer to arrive at something *it* understands, taking up more room and eating up processing time. (Programming languages are explored in detail in Appendix A.) For these reasons, a program that has to run efficiently on an end user's system must be written in a low-level language.

You should not be lulled into believing that the language facility necessary to enter the software market competitively can be quickly or conveniently acquired. Many very bright moonlighters wrote code for one or even two years before they considered entering the marketplace. Though this can be a very rewarding field, hard work, practice and patience are necessary to prepare yourself sufficiently to "break into" the business.

THOROUGHNESS

As you may have noticed in the section on case histories, the author of the word-processing program spent only one-fifth of his time creating his first working model; the rest of his time was spent in testing, debugging and improving his package. This part of programming, though it may not be as exciting, is as vital to the success of your software as are the creative aspects. Perfecting your package is the hard work of programming. I do not think it is possible to overemphasize the importance of thorough testing and debugging. You must assure your product's smooth operation in all conceivable circumstances: every operator error should be flagged and easily rectified; every step should proceed logically and easily from the one it follows. There is a natural and understandable tendency for software authors to reap the fruits of their labours as soon as possible. Resist this temptation; releasing a poorly tested program can saddle you with a reputation that is difficult to improve.

DOCUMENTATION

Documentation, the written material accompanying a program that includes operating instructions and trouble-shooting tips, has a mixed reputation in the software market, and with good reason. At worst, documentation is poorly organized, unnecessarily complex, badly written, confusing, difficult to use and almost worthless. Often, the sales of excellent products have been crippled by poor documentation. Remember, you have been immersed in your program for months; the final task—documentation—requires you to guide the users through an introduction to a program they have never seen before, allowing them to learn quickly how to use your program proficiently.

If clear and concise writing is not your forte, you may consider hiring someone who will write your documentation. At the very least, before sending your program out into the world, find a PC user who will take the program and your initial documentation draft and try to run your program. If, after a couple of hours, he is not well on his way to mastering the basics of the package, something is wrong. The importance of documentation is very great. I have included an appendix that covers the requirements for understandable documentation. I urge all potential software authors to read Appendix B carefully.

PIRACY

Unscrupulous people who make unauthorized copies of your program and either sell them or give them away are breaking the law and hurting your sales. Unfortunately, detection of software piracy is close to impossible in practice. Your program is your copyright, but few programmers rely exclusively on copyright protection. Although a stern warning of the penalties for copyright infringement cannot do any harm, many programmers choose to make piracy as difficult as possible for those pirates who are not so easily intimidated, by using a special, non-standard code to write their program, making it more difficult to copy. This sort of copy protection is usually accomplished by coding the bits onto the disk in an unorthodox way that cannot be deciphered by standard copy commands, which assume a standard bit pattern. However, programs are available that can break your bit code (e.g. *Locksmith* and *Nibbles Away*). By reading the bits themselves, they can analyze the patterns and write out the protected program in a matter of minutes in nearly all cases. At this writing, a method of applying a distinctive "fingerprint" to the disk itself has just been developed which will render a program copied onto a nonfingerprinted disk unusable. At the moment, however, this method is uncommon and there is no fail-safe way to protect your work from a dedicated pirate.

MULTIPLE VERSIONS

Naturally, the more models and operating systems your program can run on, the larger your consumer pool will be. Revisions of your initial product are required to supply more than one system, and each version will require ongoing support. Writing in a programming language such as C Language, which is noted for its "portability", can facilitate the creation of multiple versions. The lower the level of your language, the more difficult translation for additional systems will be. The three largest hardware suppliers are Apple, Tandy and IBM.

THE DISTRIBUTION NETWORK

As alluded to earlier, the sale of software is evolving toward the type of distribution employed in the music industry: the works of individuals are marketed through large professional distribution companies. While writing software has some of the characteristics of a cottage industry, the trend is away from self-marketing and toward the professional distribution. Up to now, sales were made primarily through software specialty houses. At this writing, some larger concerns are setting up software distribution; in particular, a good number of book publishers are beginning to think of software publishing as a natural extension of their present activities. Book publishers may become a major part of the software market in the future.

A definite structure has evolved to take original programs into the marketplace. The evolution of a software package from an idea to a commercial success involves an author, a publisher, who is responsible for packaging and advertising, a distributor, and the retailer. This market structure drives the price of a program up four or five times before it reaches the ultimate consumer.

FEE STRUCTURES

At this time, there is no industry-wide author contract. Software authors should be prepared to do some negotiating to arrive at their best terms. In general, authors will receive a fixed percentage of gross sales revenue, usually ranging from 10% to 20%, but occasionally falling in the larger range between 5% and 30%. Some publishers will pay authors a "sign-up" bonus whereas others will give an advance on royalties to a programmer with a good reputation in the industry, or a track record that inspires confidence. The agreement between the publisher and author spells out the duties of both, and makes some mutual determinations about the project. The two parties agree to a schedule and an eventual release date. The publisher agrees to spend a certain amount on promoting the package and on marketing, among other things, and the author accepts responsibility for delivering the program on a certain date, and for modifying, enhancing and otherwise maintaining the program.

MARKETING YOUR SOFTWARE

The key to successful software marketing is three-fold: good product design, well-timed entry into the market and a careful identification of your customer targets. Packaging and documentation are important in this market, particularly if you are writing business software, whereas graphics are vitally important to many game programs. Technical and after-sales support can help maintain the life of your product.

If you decide to sell your work through a distribution company, royalty payments will help maintain an ongoing relationship with your marketer. The number of companies purchasing and marketing PC software is growing all the time. As a guide, it is advisable to check the advertisers regularly in the many computer magazines now available. You can find out what sort of programs are available now by obtaining the following publication, which listed more than 4000 programs in a recent issue:

Software File,
EMAP Business + Computer Publications Ltd
8 Herbal Hill, London EC1

SELF-MARKETING

You may opt to sell your program yourself. There are a number of techniques you should consider to start yourself on this path. They include:

- Talking about your program to computer clubs.
- Advertising in PC magazines.
- Advertising an industry oriented program in the appropriate trade journal.
- Purchasing a mailing list from a company specializing in lists, or developing one on your own, and beginning a direct mail campaign.
- Renting booths at computer fairs and expositions.

You may also want to consider giving away "trial size" versions of your program that demonstrate how your program works in a scaled-down, presentational way; these samples can also be sold at a nominal price. If you do distribute your program in a scaled-down form, remember to make printing or storing the program or any data produced by it impossible.

Selling your documentation separately can also be a valuable part of your marketing effort. It allows your potential customer to get a close look at your programs operation and design, and determine its suitability for his operations, without requiring a purchase of the whole program. Documentation generally sells for up to £20.

AFTER-SALES SUPPORT

Customer support provided to the owners of your software not only increases the life, popularity and integrity of your program, but allows you to maximize your ongoing "relationship" with your program, creating opportunities to maximize your profit from each product. The responsible moonlighting author should be prepared to answer his customers' questions, and to correct bugs in each of his programs and forward their corrections to the customer. A common approach is one in which the vendor promises free corrections for a period of one year, after which an annual service fee is required for continued maintenance. Many moonlighters who have marketed their own programs have reported excellent results from the institution of a twenty-four hour "hot line" telephone number.

THE PROGRAMS

As mentioned at the beginning of this chapter, the software market is divided more or less between business-type software and games. The following survey of the two areas should give you, the potential moonlighter, a basic understanding of the software market.

BUSINESS SOFTWARE

The largest successes of the business software market have been achieved with generic packages, like VisiCalc, 1-2-3 and Wordstar. The authors and distributors of VisiCalc are dollar millionaires today. At this writing, the US publication *Software News* lists the five top selling programs as follows:
- Wordstar
- Multiplan
- 1-2-3
- VisiCalc
- PFS:File

Wordstar is the present state-of-the-art word-processing program, though competition is beginning to get fierce. Multiplan is a spread-sheet program, and 1-2-3 is one of the relatively new combination systems, melding the capabilities of spread-sheets, graphics packages, and database systems. I would give the prize for highest total sales to VisiCalc, with half a million programs on-line at present, disregarding the numerous VisiCalc clones on the market.

The combined functions of programs like 1-2-3 are becoming

quite popular at the moment; close study of the phenomenon of increasing the number of applications in a single package might be profitable to the talented moonlighter. Another wrinkle in the market that is becoming more common are systems that build on currently popular programs. Tax preparation programs, sometimes called *templates*, which use the spread-sheet capabilities of a program like VisiCalc, can be sold for a small fraction of a complete tax program's price. A program like Quickcode, which greatly eases the operation of the dBase II data base system, is another example of this sort of expansion program. The moonlighter without an indepth knowledge of a programming language may find the production of a system like this to be within his understanding, as they are written in the language of the package the expansion is intended for. If you develop a program like this, which is targeted for the needs of a specific industry or application, by all means investigate the resources available for marketing your program toward those specific targets.

One advantage of writing business programs is that their market is in some ways more flexible than that of games. Business programs can be updated at regular intervals, thereby expanding your market. You should develop some means of supplying enhanced versions of your programs to owners of the earlier versions. Updated versions are often sold at a nominal fee, such as £25 per program for a £300 package. Another aspect of this flexibility is the opportunity to write an enhanced version of a popular program and sell it at a lower price. Though this kind of program is one of the easiest to write, and offers an easy way into the market, there is a risk involved: someone else can do the same thing, and render your program obsolete. "Leap-frogging" in this way has often been successful, but usually for a limited time. If you write this sort of program, be sure to highlight the improvements built into your version, and the improved price-to-performance ratio. Business software also allows opportunities for moonlighters that have not mastered a low-level language of the assembly type to write straightforward applications, such as an accounting package in a high-level language like compiler BASIC.

A specific area of the business software market which may offer some of the largest opportunities to the moonlighter covers programs oriented toward a particular industry or business. If you have an intimate knowledge of the data-flow and systems requirements of a particular enterprise, you may be able to put together a specialized program, such as a dentist's accounting package, an estate agent's management system or a contractor's cost-estimation program. These types of programs cluster towards the high-priced end of the market, costing the consumer anything from £300 to more than £1000; but they may require a significant amount of after-sales support. Program systems like these can often spring from a program developed under contract to an individual user (*see* Chapter 5, Contract Programming). If you have surrendered the copyright to your program under the terms of your programming contract, you and the user must agree to some sort of joint marketing plan after his program has passed the installation and testing phase. The marketing of these types of systems is considerably simplified by the well-defined market that you are attempting to reach. Trade shows, trade journals and direct mail have proved very effective in marketing industry-specific software. Although the steadily increasing use of computers in business will bring with it a commensurate growth in software sales, it should be remembered that specialized programs will be of interest to a smaller, though more concentrated group of computer users than will be more generalized applications systems.

GAMES

Games generally have a much shorter market life than business programs, and that, coupled with the more extensive advertising required to sell games, results in a lower royalty percentage for game authors, generally paying around 5% to 10%. However, the large sales enjoyed by the popular games can more than compensate for the lower royalty percentage allotted their authors. The few writers that have achieved the largest payoffs are reported to have annual incomes of hundreds of thousands of pounds.

No one really knows what makes a popular game. Like a horse race, there will be many entries but few winners. It may take ten games on the market for your royalty income to approach your present fulltime salary. However, the most successful authors, have given up on moonlighting in order to found their own distribution companies, based on the profits reaped by their games.

A very popular game can sell 1000 to 2000 copies per month, while it is in vogue; less popular games sell perhaps two hundred per month. If you are receiving a 10% royalty on a game retailing for £15, a monthly sale of 1500 games would give you an income of £2250 per month.

In contrast to business software, which requires high-powered programming techniques, many games seem to be written by less experienced programmers. Games, like business programs, are usually written in the low-level, more efficient languages, such as assembly language, which are more difficult to learn than high-level languages like BASIC. One of the advantages claimed by proponents of the C Language is portability, the ease with which a program can be modified to run on multiple systems, and this should make it a serious contender for your game programs.

The game market is very difficult to predict. But, it should be pointed out that games seem to run in trends; destroy-the-space-ship games have been popular recently, and more educational games are just now beginning to catch on. Educational games written for younger children are also very popular at the moment. However, entertainment games are still solid in the market.

PROGRAM COPYRIGHTING

If you are still interested in becoming a moonlighting software packager, you should be aware of the complex and volatile legal situation surrounding computer programs. A number of the legal issues central to the programmer have not been settled. In the USA, quite a few cases that will set important precedents for the field are currently in litigation. In the UK the situation is rather different. On 30 January 1984 Gerald Kaufman MP asked Norman Tebbit, the UK Secretary of State for Trade and Industry, if he was satisfied that there was sufficient protection under copyright legislation to authors and publishers of computer programmes and general computer software. Mr Alex Fletcher MP, replying on behalf of Mr Tebbit replied that "Although the question has not been decided in the courts, it is widely accepted that copyright protection extends under present law to computer programs and other software. Nevertheless, to remove any doubts, the Government stated their intention in the copyright Green Paper (Cmnd 8302) published in 1981 to make it explicit in new legislation that computer programs attract copyright protection". Also, John Butcher, the British junior Industry Minister, speaking at the recent Computer Trade Association awards ceremony, confirmed that the problems of software piracy would be tackled in the current review of copyright law.

At the same time, a court decision has caused anxieties in Australia. The Federal Court overturned the ruling of a lower court that computer software programmes are not literary works, and so do not enjoy copyright. The main concern about the lower court's decision was therefore resolved. However, as at June 1984 the Australian government is examining the need to introduce legislation to amend the Copyright Act to ensure clear protection of software programmes.

CHAPTER 5

CONTRACT PROGRAMMING

EQUIPMENT:
Large memory PC, printer

EXPERTISE:
Advanced programming ability,
specialized applications

CLIENT CONTACT:
Deliver program to client per specifications;
provide training, installation and debugging, if necessary

FEES AND INVOICING:
£10 to £30 per hour, or a flat fee based on the complexity of
the assignment

EXTRAS:
Graphics, programming for mainframe, working as subcontractor.

WHAT IS CONTRACT PROGRAMMING?

A moonlighter who enters the contract programming field will write
original software, or modify existing software, under contract to
an individual client. The contract will cover systems specifications,
scheduling, and fees. Unlike the program packager discussed in
Chapter Four, who designs a program and then tries to sell it, the
contract programmer sells his expertise and programming skill to an
individual looking for software that will perform a specific set of
tasks unique to his business. This type of work is similar to Consulting (see Chapter Six), except that the moonlighter in contract programming uses his analysis of a client's operations to design a piece
of software, rather than to make recommendations, and has certain
affinities to Systems Houses (Chapter Seven), but with hardware
acquisition lying outside the moonlighter's responsibilities. This
chapter, and the two that follow, can be read in conjunction with one

another to give the moonlighter an overview of the opportunities inherent to thorough and indepth computer expertise.

In contrast to the preceding three chapters, which covered Freelance Writing, Service Bureaux and Program Packages, the material that follows involves advanced skills and extensive contact with small businessmen and others who have a serious commitment to the use of the personal computer in their professional lives. In considering contract programming, and other areas requiring extensive client contact, the moonlighter should carefully evaluate his background and suitability for the work *before* committing time and resources in an attempt to enter the field. The next section should help you to begin your self-evaluation.

IS IT FOR YOU?

I have broken down this question into a number of distinct areas, each of which should help guide you as you consider the prospect of a moonlighting career in contract programming.

PROGRAMMING

Proficiency in at least one, and preferably more than one, of the low-level, more efficient languages, such as assembler and C Language, is vital. It should be self-evident that considerable practice and study of programming will be necessary before you can comfortably bill yourself as a professional programmer capable of designing a system that can efficiently handle the data processing needs of an entire business, or an operational segment of a business. Programming requires long stretches of concentration and considerable attention to detail. If you feel this is beyond your powers, you may be happier considering some of the other areas of computer moonlighting I discuss.

BUSINESS ANALYSIS

You must have the ability to analyze a business situation and convert information-flow requirements into program specifications. Familiarity with the structure and function of information systems provides the moonlighting contract programmer with enormous advantages.

CAREFUL DEFINITION OF TASKS

A special section in this chapter has been devoted to the preparation of the proposal that forms the basis of your relationship with your client. The importance of preproposal analysis and the preparation of an accurate and thorough proposal, defining precisely what is to be delivered, cannot be overemphasized. The proposal usually becomes the contract under which you work, so attention to this process exactly limits what you agree to produce, and is vitally important to you, the moonlighter, who must provide an estimate of the time required or quote a flat-fee bid.

WORKING UNDER CONTRACT

The contract programmer must be able to develop a detailed project plan before he begins work; and he must then use this plan to design his proposal. Learning to work under contract involves a realistic evaluation of your abilities and the time available to you to complete work according to a schedule that is satisfactory to your client. Many people who have never worked under contract make the mistake of underestimating the time needed to do a job under consideration, in an attempt to make themselves more attractive to their clients. This often results in panic striken late-night work sessions or reduction of the moonlighter's hourly wages, or both. Being reliable about deadlines is one of the most important habits necessary to earn a good reputation as an independent contractor: nothing annoys a client more than seeing a mutually agreed upon project milestone (the completion of a preliminary task or evaluation) pass by without delivery of the goods.

CLIENT CONTACT

All form of moonlighting that involve contractual agreements should result in the development of close business working relationships. If you are not comfortable in working with other people, occasionally in stressful situations, or placing yourself in a situation requiring negotiations, you may have trouble in an area like contract programming. The close ties you must develop with your client will usually have to be maintained for a number of months.

WHO HIRES CONTRACT PROGRAMMERS?

Most of your potential clients will be small businessmen who need certain software capabilties to manage their businesses effectively.

However, they cannot buy packaged programs off the shelf to fulfill their software needs, and are not willing, or able, to develop their own programs in-house. However, they have often already established a computer presence in their places of business, can recognize the advantages of obtaining specialized software and are willing to pay for its development.

The cost of commissioning the development of original software far exceeds any other method of program acquisition, running eight to ten times in excess of packaged application costs. A packaged payroll system may run from £350 to £1000, whereas a custom developed payroll package could easily cost more than £4000. Your client can generally justify this added expense in one of two ways: there are no adequate commercial programs available; or, the savings or increased earnings attributable to custom tailoring are very likely to return the additional expenditure quickly.

YOU AND YOUR CLIENT

Your initial contact with your client will involve a discussion of your credentials, the background you have had in this type of work, a discussion of the clients needs and an analysis of his application. As a result of the first discussions and meetings, you will develop a proposal.

THE PROPOSAL

Although there are as yet no industry standards for these proposals, you should consider including the following items in your proposal:
- A resumé of your qualifications.
- References.
- A detailed description of the software you are to write, broken down into modules, if the length and complexity demands it. Detail is extremely important in this section, as it usually becomes the contractual definition of what you agree to produce. It should include the following information:

Hardware required to run the program, including memory size and peripherals;

The operating system to be used;

Programming language you will use;

Other software systems to be interfaced with your program;

Input characteristics, including data volume and formats;

Operational specifications, such as run times;

Output specifications, including reports and format.

● Total cost, either per hour, per hour to an agreed limit, or a flat fee; and a payment schedule.

● Project completion schedule with milestones for specific modules.

● Description of documentation.

● Training to be provided, post-installation support, and fee arrangements for same.

● Ownership of software copyright and marketing rights, including any joint marketing arrangement.

● An agreement by you that any information you obtain relating to the client's operations will be kept confidential and will not be used outside the context of the agreement.

● A time limit to the validity of the proposal, usually 60 days.

● A statement of limited warranty that guarantees that the system will perform according to agreed upon specifications, and that this is the full extent of your obligations and responsibilities.

Prepare two signed copies of the document for your client (be sure to keep a copy for yourself in case of loss etc.), have him review it and discuss any changes he suggests. Once all terms are agreed to, have him sign one copy and return it to you. This document, signed by both you and the client, now becomes the legally binding initial contract and authorizes you to proceed with your work. However, most contract programmers prepare additional documents once this agreement is reached, and incorporate them into the contract. These documents serve to narrowly define the contracted program and are summarized in the next section.

SUPPORTING DOCUMENTS

With the initial contract in hand, you should begin the design of your software by developing documentation that includes a system narrative, detailing the logical structure of the program, and a system-level flow diagram. When these documents are complete (probably the first milestone of the schedule portion of your initial contract) and have been reviewed and approved by your client, these documents are incorporated into the contract by the signatures of the two parties, providing a highly detailed description of the software to be produced. After these initial phases are complete, you should begin the actual coding and testing of the program, as well as preparing the final documentation. (The importance of documentation is so great that I have included in Appendix B a complete discussion of guidelines for its preparation, which the moonlighter should review carefully.)

It is to your benefit to make your proposal as general as possible while remaining within the bounds of responsibility and professionalism. It is important that you have the flexibility to amend your original plans should you run into unexpected difficulties, or devise an alternative strategy once you begin the actual coding. Most clients do not expect rigid adherence to the details of your plan, as long as the specifications and deadlines are met, but will naturally want as much detail as possible in the proposal. A forthright discussion of the difficulties of programming will greatly ease the establishment of a working relationship and promote mutual respect and trust.

COPYRIGHT

One negotiating point that occasionally creates an awkward situation involves the ownership of the program copyright. If there is a chance that you may want to market software written under contract, it is vital that you make detailed provisions in your contract concerning marketing rights. There are three possibilities for copyright disposition: you own the copyright completely as the author; your client owns it as the one who commissioned it; or there is a joint ownership agreement. If you make no provision for these rights in the contract, your client will enjoy full rights to the program you write. If you believe that you may have the opportunity to market the program after the expiration of your contract, and your client has no interest in entering the software marketing business, it is possible that he will surrender the copyright to you as one provision of your contract. The chances are, though, that he will want some sort of payment for giving up the rights to the program, such as a reduction in your fee. If you enter into a joint ownership agreement with your client, such as sharing marketing costs and profits, it should be written carefully and explained in detail. Remember that some of the most successful packaged programs were originally developed under contract, and that an original program, or one that serves a previously unexploited market, could be worth a large amount of money to its owner.

FEES

How you arrive at an amount for your fee, and the method of payment you choose, is influenced by a number of factors. Although you can be paid either at an hourly rate, at an hourly rate to a certain upper limit, or a flat fee, you should strive for a final fee of £15 to £30 per hour. Naturally, you should be able to confidently estimate the number of hours a specific project will take. Many clients are primarily interested in the "bottom line", and prefer either a maximum figure or a flat fee. Of course, these methods of determining your fee involve considerably more risk than if you were being paid a simple hourly wage, particularly if the application you are trying to give an estimate on is beyond your previous experience or the experience of other programmers you may be familiar with.

Under no circumstances should your fee be tied to the anticipated savings or increased earnings predicted from the institution of your software system. This is unethical; these savings or earnings may not materialize, for reasons completely beyond your control.

NUTS AND BOLTS

If your personal computer is not the same model as your client's, you must gain access to a computer that matches his. Writing a program on a system that does not match the system of your end user will create tremendous conversion problems, which is something you should avoid at all costs. You might consider approaching your client with a request to use his system for program writing; but keep in mind that your professionalism might be called into question if you can't arrange access on your own system.

Once your system has been written, never take your client's software off-line until the new program has been on-line for a time sufficient to guarantee its error-free operation. The time needed for this will vary, but , at the least, it should be two or three operational cycles without error. For example, run it for several weeks before you cut loose the back-up of your client's original system.

MARKETING

Avenues for making your services known include:
- Advertising in newspapers, in computer magazines and on cable television, when available.
- Personal contacts and the distribution of business cards.
- Direct mail to individuals likely to hire a contract programmer.
- Freelance articles written to highlight your experience and expertise.
- References from your previous clients.

- Membership of a professional organization.
- Contact with computer retailers.

If you have experience in, or knowledge of, a particular business field, you should make a concerted effort to advertise your services to the people in that field. The marketing problems of contract programming are relatively straightforward. More imaginative and powerful marketing techniques are available in some of the other moonlighting areas. Consulting, in particular, demands a more extensive range of marketing activities, and the interested moonlighter should turn to the discussion of "Marketing Yourself" in Consulting, Chapter Six (page 103) for techniques that might be profitably modified for use by contract programmer.

SPECIAL PROBLEMS AND OPPORTUNITIES

The first hurdle to cross when selling yourself as a moonlighting contract programmer will be the client's reluctance to hire a part-time programmer when fulltime programmers are available as well. In the beginning, your only answer to such an objection will be to offer a lower fee. Your primary object is extra income, but you do have a certain flexibility in your fee structure, because, unlike a company that supplies computer programming, you do not have the financial obligations of overheads and fringe benefits, nor do you have to charge fees to cover your living expenses should you go without work for any length of time. Of course, an in-depth knowledge of a particular application and excellent recommendations from previous clients can ease your potential customer's reluctance to hire a moonlighter. As I stressed before, *always* let your client know that you are operating on a moonlighting basis.

Although the demands on your time in this moonlighting area are not as extensive as in the client-contact fields covered in Chapters Six and Seven, you should keep in mind that at least a portion of your activities as a moonlighting contract programmer must be carried out during business hours. Installation and training, as well as calls for post-installation support, are most likely to cause time conflicts with your 9-to-5 job. Flexibility in time commitments at your office are an important ingredient for success in this aspect of computer moonlighting.

You should expect to encounter heavy competition from solidly established programming companies when entering this field, particularly from those with an industry-specific orientation. Competition is also likely from those computer retailers who maintain a staff of contract programmers to handle their customers specialized software needs. Excellent work, ingenuity, patience, and a few lucky breaks will assist you in the battle to build up a solid reputation in the programming field.

SUBCONTRACTING

Contract programmers who have achieved a certain level of success may find that they are offered more work than they can realistically accept. Subcontracting for an over-burdened contract programmer is one of the best ways to break into the field for the beginning moonlighter. Typically, the prime contractor will seek out the potential clients, make the sales, then turn to you for the actual programming. He may confine himself to seeking out new business, or he may prepare the proposal and the supporting documentation, leaving the actual code writing to you. Typically, the prime contractor will retain 15% to 30% of the total fee and pass the rest on to you, depending, of course, on the individual circumstances of the project, and the negotiated agreement you and he reach. Subcontracting is especially helpful to the programmer who has not yet established a reputation, and to the programmer who does not possess a large amount of business acumen. Though subcontracting provides an excellent opportunity, and relieves you of administrative headaches, there are also some problems peculiar to the area to which you should give careful attention.

Since the prime contractor maintains direct contact with the client, you will usually have to work through him, at one remove from the client and his operations. As a subcontractor, you must keep both the client and the prime contractor happy, which can sometimes be a burden. For this reason, it is a good idea to ensure that communications lines are open and effective. On a more practical level, there is the question of payment. You are paid by the prime contractor, not the client, so you must negotiate an agreement with the prime contractor and, if at all possible, commit the agreement to writing. It is always best to confine your agreement to a relationship between yourself and the prime contractor. Because you will actually write the program to the prime contractor's specifications, your agreement should contain no references to the client. If your prime contractor is not paid, due to some reason beyond your control, but you have maintained your end of the bargain, you have the right to be paid, and that right should be contractually binding.

THE FUTURE

The market for contract programming will continue to be solid, but in the long run I do not think it will keep pace with the PC market as a whole, due to advances in the operating capabilities of commercially available hardware and software. As software becomes increasingly easy to use, and more and more specialized packages can be obtained off-the-shelf, the need for customized programming will be minimal. As hardware costs go down and efficiency increases, the demand for software efficiency is likely to decrease, making more operations economical even though the PC uses less efficient software.

Personal computer users will, in the future, still require custom-developed software, especially those whose operational peculiarities require specialized treatment. Sufficient work will be available in this field to ensure its viability as a moonlighting option for quite some time to come.

CONSULTING

EQUIPMENT:
PC

EXPERTISE:
In-depth knowledge of computer applications,
hardware and software.

CLIENT CONTACT:
Extensive survey of proposed application;
delivery of final report;
contractual agreement.

FEES AND INVOICING:
£10–30 per hour or flat fee;
bill every other week or on delivery of report.

EXTRAS:
Word processing, vendor contact, follow-up,
contract programming.

THE ROLE OF
THE MOONLIGHTING CONSULTANT

A computer consultant is usually hired to help solve a specific problem about computers and their application, or to provide information and analysis concerning a particular aspect of computing. A consultant may be called upon to address a wide range of concerns. He might be asked to provide any number of things, from a survey of state-of-the-art accounting software to recommendations on the installation of an entire hardware and software system. A client outlines an area of concern, and the consultant, after study and analysis, prepares a report summarizing the problem, reports his findings, and makes his recommendations. Consultants are certainly not more intelligent than anybody else, but they have usually developed expertise in a few specific areas. Generally, a person that lacks either extensive knowledge of computers, a particular computer application, or who cannot spare the time and resources to do the necessary research in-house is likely to turn to a consultant for assistance.

Consulting demands a fairly in-depth knowledge of personal computing hardware, software and operating capabilities. If a client asks you what sort of system might best track his inventory, or how his existing system might best be upgraded, you must have access to a large amount of background information and a number of computing techniques to provide a meaningful answer. In this chapter, I will suggest some directions you can pursue to gain expertise likely to help you compete in the consulting market.

Moonlighting as a consultant is a very different prospect than the part-time computer opportunities previously discussed in this book. In the other areas, you were selling a finished product—a program or article—or a specific, essentially mechanical, service. Here, we are exploring an area in which you are offering a less tangible product— your experience, expertise and judgment. The intangible nature of your product has far-reaching consequences for both the demands of the work and the techniques necessary to successfully market yourself. No matter how your name comes to the attention of someone who needs help answering a computer related question, his inevitable first comment will be, "who is this, and why should I give him the kind of money he's asking for?" Because the only tangible product expected from you is a report, perhaps six pages long, the question is more than reasonable. This is one area where advice is *not* cheap. Toward the end of this chapter, I'll discuss some strategies for letting the right people know who you are. But first, let's discuss who these "right people" are likely to be.

WHO HIRES CONSULTANTS?

As you may remember from Chapter One, the personal computer "revolution" has left a number of small businessmen intrigued and, at the same time wary. Although they recognize the potential improvements in efficiency and customer service available to them, they may have heard a few horror stories as well. Many potential computer owners know little or nothing about the equipment available, or how their day-to-day operations are likely to change with the introduction of computers. Because they are not in the habit of committing significant amounts of capital or making drastic operational changes without a complete understanding of the questions involved, they are naturally anxious to seek out the assistance of someone well versed in the intricacies of computing.

As a consultant in personal computer systems, your clients will most likely be drawn from the ranks of small businesses, simply because most individuals have neither the resources not the need to engage your services, and most large commercial concerns are either interested in large systems, or will hire their own staff of data-processing personnel. This is not to say that it is impossible to find work as a consultant to a large company, but simply that, on a moonlighting basis, the small business is your best bet. However, keep in mind that you can consult to an entire company, or a particular department, such as Accounting or Marketing, within a larger operation.

TYPES OF CLIENTS

The actual capabilities of the personal computer are the primary factors in influencing the *type* of business likely to need your consulting services. Computers are designed to store, retrieve and analyze information. Therefore, you should be looking for businesses that must handle large volumes of information that are fairly well structured and easily put into a computer system.

ACCOUNTING FIRMS: A small accounting firm is one instructive example. The work that an accounting firm does is almost exclusively data management. A series of numbers, modified by a limited array of definitions, keeps a running numeric picture of the clients' financial situations. Excellent packaged accounting software is presently available and, with some programming ability and accounting background, it should not be difficult to write original, or modify packaged, software for your particular client. A computer system can also be designed that will "flag" time-dependent accounting tasks, such as indicating when certificates must be "rolled over" or cashed, or when quarterly tax statements are due, a week or two in advance. A small firm, say, with twenty clients, would be an ideal candidate for installation of a system of personal computers you could design and recommend.

RETAILERS AND WHOLESALERS: Retailers and wholesalers—shops, timber yards, heating oil distributors, contractors, to name a few—offer other opportunities to the moonlighting consultant. Their inventories must be tracked, information on particular products and customers must be readily available, credit limits must be policed, invoices must be prepared, sales trends must be identified. All these operations cry out for computerized management techniques.

PROFESSIONALS: Many small companies are aggressively entering the computer age. Also, doctors, and most other professionals, are just beginning to realize the tremendous advantages even straightforward systems can offer their businesses.

OTHER CLIENTS: Remember, businesses quite removed from extensive numeric concerns may also profitably computerize their operations. Any firm that must issue invoices, maintain a mailing list or send form letters would see a drastic reduction in repetitive, boring and inaccurate clerical work with the installation of a personal computing system. Many book, magazine and newspaper publishers marvel that they ever functioned without their word processing networks. Computers are also useful in maintaining files that need constant updating, such as the reservation lists kept by travel agencies. In addition, nearly every aspect of present-day sales and marketing activities are easily computerized.

WHAT YOU ALREADY KNOW...

You should keep in mind that many of the most successful computer consultants use their knowledge of a particular business, acquired before they were introduced to computers, as the cornerstone of their new consulting businesses. Your present career, past employment experiences, contact with a family business, or any other contact you have had with a particular business or organization that may profit from the use of computers, might well be the springboard you need into consulting. Keep in mind that many potential clients will be more comfortable dealing with a consultant with intimate exposure to their type of business and a working knowledge of computers, than a computer expert trying to apply his knowledge to an essentially unfamiliar operation. Although previous experience with the sort of business you attempt to consult to is not a prerequisite you should consider what sort of expertise you now possess that could be exploited as a consultant to a particular field. A combination of specialized business knowledge and a thorough understanding of personal computers could be a winning combination in the consulting market.

...AND WHAT YOU CAN LEARN

One habit that would be helpful to form involves consistent attempts to increase your knowledge of business and business practices. As a consultant, you are a temporary partner to a commercial concern; it would pay for you to know as much as possible about various aspects of business, both for a project in hand, and in order to open areas previously closed to you. Talk to as many people as possible about the nuts-and-bolts operations of their jobs and businesses. Read trade journals and other material pertaining to businesses you are acquainted with or in which you are interested. Remember that everything you know or learn may have an eventual impact on your work as a consultant. Anything more than a layman's knowledge or common sense—familiarity with a particular supply mechanism or tax structure—can do much to ease the "Who is this?" concerns, particularly in an initial meeting. A client assumes he must explain his particular operation to you, but is considerably less willing to explain his entire industry.

BASIC COMPUTER KNOW-HOW

Assuming you have sufficient acquaintance with a particular business to perform your consulting assignment, attention shifts to the complementary requirement—a working knowledge of personal computers.

YOUR OWN PC

There are a number of ways to gain this knowledge. Though not essential, perhaps the most important tool is your own personal computer. Working with a computer of your own gives you hands-on experience that is irreplaceable in your consulting work. It is necessary to know how PC's work, what they're capable of doing, what they're incapable of doing, which things are simple to accomplish, and which are likely to be frustrating. One of your foremost challenges as a consultant, particularly if your client is "computer illiterate", is ensuring that the transition from a manual to an automated office is as smooth as possible. Letting the client know what to expect, how to instruct his employees, and what to do if something goes wrong—advice that is likely to be used long after you're gone—is vitally important; meeting this challenge has a dominant impact on how your client speaks to others of your consulting job. "No headaches" is by far the most valuable praise.

READING UP

Published information can provide a wealth of data on specific hardware and software products. Personal computer magazines publish software reviews on a regular basis and are thoroughly objective. Many of the personal computing periodicals, and the more general interest computing periodicals, are full of information vital to the moonlighting consultant; subscriptions to several of these suited to your personal taste and needs, should be considered a necessary business expense.

ADVERTISING

Advertisements also provide good sources of both hardware and software information. Naturally, you must bear in mind that an advertisement aims to sell a product, so you won't get the other side of the story. Ads in magazines provide one source of information; more complete information, often accompanied by specifications, can be obtained in the form of promotional brochures available at most computer stores.

THE COMPUTER STORE: A SAFE HAVEN

Retail outlets can be useful in other ways as well. They provide a large concentration of knowledgeable and objective computer enthusiasts. If you find a shop that offers competitive prices, good after-sales service and employees you trust, it would make sense to cultivate a relationship there. The staff salesmen can often fill you in on new products and help you if you run into unfamiliar territory; in return, recommending a trustworthy retail outlet to your client can be a perfectly legitimate part of your final report. Computer stores are often willing to provide a demonstration for your client, an ideal opportunity for your client to "test drive" different parts of his potential system. Remember to give the shop adequate notice and let them know exactly which equipment you'd like to demonstrate. Also, schedule more time than you think you'll need, as no one likes to be rushed through an introduction to a new system, especially a computer novice.

SOFTWARE AND DOCUMENTATION

If you are interested in a specific piece of software, you should always inspect its documentatioon. Many suppliers will sell documentation separately for this purpose, usually for £15 or £25 per program. Always check at a computer store that sells the software first, as they will frequently let you look through the documentation at no cost. Some suppliers will also allow you to run their software at home on a trial basis.

CURRENT USERS

A final source of information for both hardware and software, one of the most valuable to the moonlighting consultant, is the collected reactions of current users. Because the products under consideration are usually on-line and functioning in a business environment, user reactions can provide confirmation to your initial conclusions or lead you to re-evaluate your recommendation. The supplier or manufacturer may provide you with a list of current users, and user reports can be obtained through the many computer clubs now in existence.

Once you have a marketable level of experience in personal computing, how might your client ask you to employ that hard-won knowledge? In consulting you will find two major areas where your help is needed. The first requires a report outlining a new system installation recommendation, a service a consultant provides to a client who does not have a computer system and would like to know if acquiring one would be advisable. The second kind of consultant report outlines how a client's existing system might be improved, modified or expanded.

YOU AND YOUR CLIENT

When a client asks a consultant to make a recommendation concerning the installation of a new system, he generally wants to know two things: whether automating his office makes sound business sense and, if it does, what combination of hardware and software most completely meets his needs, within a certain price range. This type of consulting affords the most latitude, as the moonlighter is not forced to work around an existing system that may or may not have been well designed. However, this latitude carries with it a larger set of concerns you must consider.

NOT EVERYONE NEEDS COMPUTERS

One of the most important considerations you must keep in mind, if you take on this sort of consulting assignment, involves your client's preconceptions about computers and their abilities. Many, perhaps nearly all, businessmen with little or no computer experience have a distorted impression of how large a difference computers will make in their enterprises. Your client is likely to see a computer system as a magic wand that will eliminate waste, inaccuracy and all avoidable business losses. Although a computer *is* a powerful tool, it is the guiding hand of the craftsman, rather than the tool itself, that determines the final result. The most important part of your job is the survey of your client's operation (the "Findings" section of your final report). You must completely understand the portion of your client's business under consideration for automation. Of course, you will often find that computers would be an appropriate addition to his day-to-day data-management activities. Occasionally, though, you will determine that the problem lies elsewhere—in illogical organization, inefficient individual processes, poor data flow or poor communication channels—and that the expense of a computer system can not really be justified. Simply cleaning up the present operation may solve your client's problem. If you believe this is the case, it is in your best interest, and your client's, to indicate the problem in your report. A consultant who regularly recommends expensive computer systems that offer little or no improvements, or make things even more unmanageable, quickly earns a poor reputation, even if his client's operation, and not the system he recommends, is at fault. Of course, there is no reason not to identify trouble spots in a client's organization *and* make a system recommendation, as long as you clearly indicate what the computers can and cannot accomplish.

THE EXISTING SYSTEM

A client with an existing system will most likely desire specific advice on how to accomplish a particular end. He may desire to add another part of his operation to the system, expand the system to take on additional duties, or replace or modify his present complement of software. Occasionally, a client will ask for a more general analysis: how might this system be used to better advantage, what sort of additions or modifications would be most useful, are his employees properly trained, and the like. In this sort of consulting, the moonlighter must examine both the existing system and its design, *and* the ways in which the system is actually being used.

THE SURVEY

No matter which sort of consulting work is asked for, it is vitally important that the consultant completely understands his client's operation. This is accomplished through a detailed survey of the particular aspects of the client's business under consideration, and is usually the most time-consuming portion of the consultant's task. Any source of information can be important. As I mentioned earlier, a comprehensive understanding of the client's type of enterprise is critical to your success. Any written information about the department you are examining, such as procedural manuals, instructions, rules and training materials should be closely studied. Statistical data, such as turnaround times, quality control summaries and sales figures can be quite instructive. You should always try, if it is at all possible, to talk to your client's employees; the people actually doing the work as well as department heads and supervisors. It is in these interviews that you can discover how the work is actually accomplished, where nodes of frustration exist, and the improvements most desired by the people who will be using the computers you may recommend. A consultant that invests time and care in a very thorough survey will recommend systems, both hardware and software, or system modifications that will be easily integrated into his client's business procedures and help to solve the problems on hand. Attention to this aspect of consulting will have an enormous positive impact on your client's evaluation of your work.

A note of caution is called for at this point in the discussion. As a consultant, you may occasionally be placed in a somewhat awkward position. You will almost always be hired by the owner of the company or someone quite high in the heirarchy of the company. He may or may not be on good terms with those working under him. Even in the friendliest offices, there may be understandable resentment from some people at being scrutinized by an outsider, or suspicion that your recommendations will make their work harder or more complicated, or may cost someone his or her job. If you land in the middle of some unpleasant office politics, remember that you may occasionally be unable to defuse it. Remain objective and tread carefully. Pay attention to the nuances of people's reaction to your presence. Remember that you will be involved with each company temporarily, while the people you meet and work with must live with each other, and the results of your work, long after you have left. You will not often run into problems of this nature, but responsibility and sensitivity are always called for.

CHECKING BACK

After your survey, but before preparing your recommendations, *always* return to your client so you and he can discuss your evaluation of his business and the problem needing attention. Nothing is guaranteed to displease everyone involved more than an entire consulting report based on an uncorrected misunderstanding.

THE REPORT

Once your initial survey is complete, you should develop your final report. As I mentioned earlier, your report should be approximately six pages in length, and will consist of a summary of your client's question to you, the results of your survey and your recommendations. The report should be typed, double spaced, include a title page and be presented in an attractive cover.

YOUR RECOMMENDATIONS

Because no two computer applications are exactly alike, your judgement and expertise must mould your recommendations to fit the needs of your client. However, whether you are working with an existing system, or starting from scratch, there are some general system guidelines you should keep in mind in systems recommendations.

SYSTEM COSTS. Your client may or may not have given you a budget with which to work. It is, of course, your client's responsibility to weigh the costs and benefits and make a final decision on what to purchase. Your responsibility is to give him an accurate report on the most cost-effective options available to him and recommend one, with an analysis. Some consultants, whether they have been given a target price or not, provide two or three rated recommendations, giving the price and capabilities of each. You should also alert your client to *all* costs he is likely to incur, including installation, training materials, maintenance and the like. Estimates are perfectly appropriate, when necessary, but should be labelled as such. The option to lease or rent, rather than buy, should also be investigated.

CONVENIENCE. Is the software user-friendly? Can the computer be used by someone with little or no experience? Is the hardware well-designed and easy to use? Is maintenance likely to be a problem? Is the system easy to trouble-shoot? Are these instructional materials and good owner's manuals available? The answers to all these questions should influence your recommendations.

FLEXIBILITY. Most business systems will, at one time or another, need to be expanded. How easily a particular system can be modified to changing business conditions is often an important factor in both hardware and software selection. How many program packages are compatible with a given system? Is there a range of convenient outboard equipment, such as additional memory and printers, available? Is the source code for software available to allow program modifications? Is the documentation adequate?

SERVICE. How extensive and reliable is the vendor support? How long have the pieces of the system been on the market, and how many are currently in use? What sort of warranties are available from the manufacturer? Do current users report difficulty obtaining prompt, thorough, competent maintenance? Again, recommending a system that is a constant headache is one of the hidden dangers of consulting. Attention to service and reliability factors offers the only insurance against this.

DELIVERING THE REPORT, AND AFTER

You should meet with your client one last time when you deliver your report. Sit down with him, discuss your recommendations, answer his questions. Clients appreciate personal, patient attention from their consultants almost as much as excellent recommendations. You should also make it clear that you are available to answer client questions after your report is completed. It is also a good idea to contact your client several months after your report is delivered. Checking up on the system, fine tuning its use, is often an easy way to raise your stature as a responsible consultant. It is also an excellent way to obtain an additional consulting contract, should your client feel prepared to expand or modify his system.

CLIENT RELATIONSHIP

Now that you have an idea of the work a consultant does, I will turn to the nuts-and-bolts mechanics of the moonlighting consultant's relationship with his client. First of all, you should *always* let your client know you are working as a consultant on a moonlighting basis. Sooner or later, the masquerade of fulltime status would fail, with unpredictable but probably unpleasant results. Of course, it is not necessary to emphasize your part-time status either. Mention it, assure the client it will pose no problem whatsoever, and turn to other matters. After that, be on time for appointments, and never do less than your best for a client. Remember that consulting is cumulative; each job improves your track-record for the next assignment.

As you may have assumed by now, working as part-time consultant does require a certain flexibility in your fulltime job. Meetings, and your survey, usually must take place during business hours at your client's office. If available, long lunches are a boon. Occasionally, holidays must be used. Working nonstandard hours, or a nonstandard week, is ideal. A client may be willing to meet you after hours, but don't count on it.

THE INITIAL MEETING

There is a certain professionalism involved in consulting. After seeing one of your advertisements, receiving a mailing or meeting you in some way, a client will contact you and indicate an interest in your services. You should meet him, either in his office or for lunch, and discuss the details of your service, his computer questions and the schedule he has in mind.

THE PROPOSAL

The question of payment is important, and also a bit complex. Do not, under any circumstances, allow your payment to be directly tied to the money spent on your recommendation. Being paid a percentage of the eventual purchase is unprofessional and can lead to suspicion that you are including unnecessary equipment in your recommendation. You should be paid like any other professional, for services rendered. Depending on your taste, and the situation, you may be paid by the hour, a flat fee, or hourly with a certain price ceiling. It is advisable to indicate a fee only after the initial face-to-face encounter. You need a general idea as to the scope of the job, its complexity and projected time commitment before quoting a price; and your potential client should meet you, form an opinion of your abilities, and evaluate your credentials before considering a particular fee schedule. A moonlighting consultant new to the business should expect to work at a bargain price until he has achieved an impressive record of consulting jobs. The rock bottom consulting fee is £10 per hour. Experienced consultants charge £25 to £30 per hour, or more. It is a good idea to have an absolute minimum hourly rate below which you will not work. Since it is almost always impossible to work fulltime and do more than one consulting job at a time, every project you take on takes you out of the market until it is completed.

After your initial meeting, if you have reached a verbal agreement about your services, you should send your client a letter. Many consultants let this letter serve as the contract as well. Summarize your meeting, describe in detail what you propose to do for your client, and include your arrangements for payment. Restate the scheduling agreed to by your client. It is important that this document, whether contained in the confirmation letter or included in a separate contract, covers the *entire* agreement between you and your client. While it is always more pleasant if your client-consultant relationship is casual and flexible, if there is a dispute of some kind it is vital that both parties have the ability to refer to the same document, rather than to verbal agreements that can be misremembered or misconstrued.

There are two paragraphs that you should always incorporate into your written agreements. The first should indicate that you will proceed in good faith and with your best efforts, but should make no guarantees beyond delivery of a report and accept no liability for any consequential damages based on your recommendations. The second should simply state that the document in question, and its attachments (which should be numbered), constitute the entire agreement between you and your client, and that no other statements, written or verbal, will be considered part of the agreement, nor shall they be binding. Remember that this is a business relationship, and there is nothing distrustful or unsavoury about putting your agreement in writing. Make three copies of this document, sign them, and send two to your client with instructions to sign one and return it to you if it is acceptable to him. If there is some problem, meet with him again and attempt to clear it up. Such a letter, signed by both of you, is a perfectly legal and binding contract.

GETTING PAID: You should bill your client at the end of the job, or, if it is a long-term relationship, at the end of every other week. Each invoice should be submitted on your letterhead stationary, dated, have a description of services rendered (for example, consulting work, 1/1/84 to 14/1/84: 20 hours) and an amount to be paid. These invoices are necessary to your client for tax purposes, in addition to lending your enterprise a professional touch.

MARKETING YOURSELF

If this sort of moonlighting sounds intriguing and promising, you will want to know how to sell your consulting services. As I mentioned earlier, the intangible nature of your product has the single largest effect on your marketing techniques. Before I discuss specific forums for advertising, let me outline some general principles.

Most importantly, you are selling yourself—your expertise, judgment, experience and professionalism. Your potential client must be convinced that you will do a responsible, thorough and knowledgeable job before he will hire you as a consultant. Appearances matter. Yours should exude a professional air. Wear a suit and tie. Your adverts and letters should breathe "trustworthy" and "independent businessman". In addition to *being* a professional expert, you should look and act the part. Accept your position as a knowledgeable professional in an area where your client has amateur status.

Remember that consulting is a cumulative enterprise. After your first job, you are not only selling your professionalism, but your reputation. After completing a consulting job, ask your client to refer you to others that might profit from your services. Always ask if potential clients may contact your client for a reference. This is an additional reason to make follow-up visits. If, for some reason, your client becomes unhappy with your job, you should know it before someone contacts him for a reference. Occasionally, a client will be dissatisfied; it could be for any number of reasons. Obviously, do not use such a client as a reference. If you can't patch things up, simply chalk it up to experience and move on. Always keep in mind that your reputation is your greatest asset. Supply each potential client with a resumé that includes a detailed account of your best work for previous clients. Explain what you recommended and the concrete improvements their adoption made in the client's operations. Urge your potential client to contact one or two references for confirmation. Remember, this is one of the best reasons to be sensitive and attentive to each client's needs, both during and after your consulting work.

MAKING CONTACT

Referrals and advertising *are* important, but personal contacts are a proven way to get new business. Talk to people, *however* you make their acquaintance, about their business, your consulting work and personal computers. If you meet someone that may hire you, or refer you to a friend that might hire you, ask for their card and ring them in the next day or so, before your meeting recedes in his memory. You will find, with surprising frequency, that a chance encounter can be transformed into a valuable relationship. If you have pride and confidence in your work, you should have no qualms about suggesting your services to someone that could make good use of them.

SPECIALIZATION

As discussed earlier, it is important that you exploit your noncomputer experience in placing yourself in the market as a specialist. If you have experience in health services, the law, travel agencies, or some other promising industry, by all means focus your efforts in that area. Although your services may come to the attention of fewer people, those that do hear of your enterprise will be more likely to get in touch with a consultant who has in-depth knowledge of their field than a newcomer. Don't try to be everything to everyone; the market is glutted with consultants that promise anything to anybody. Remember that there is no reason to confine yourself to a single speciality. Make your more general skills known in a more general market; focus information about your specific specialities in appropriate segments of the market.

ADVERTISING

There are a large number of forums for your advertising. Computer magazines often sell classified ads to all manner of computer professionals. These ads are often reasonably priced and can be very effective. If you advertise in a national magazine, be sure to identify the geographical area in which you will accept work. Local newspapers and some regional magazines take classified advertising for professional services. Investigate these publications as marketing tools. Some newspapers print special sections for computer services, often on one particular day of the week. This is a relatively inexpensive way to reach those looking for specific computer services. National general interest publications sometimes take classified ads, but cannot provide a high concentration of readers likely to be interested in your service. Finally, if you do specialize, seek out the trade journal(s) directed toward that industry. Nearly all such magazines carry the type of advertising useful to you, and many are quite willing to accept a freelance article outlining your particular area of computer expertise, or a specific data-management technique you have developed. These outlets deliver the most specialized readers to your advertisements, and you may find that you are the only computer consultant available in your particular field, or one of a small handful.

DIRECT MAIL

Direct mail is a powerful marketing tool. Put together a brochure and send it to a number of firms likely to use your consulting services. If at all possible, find the name of a particular person, such as a managing director, department head, or other manager likely to have direct control over the area to which you would like to offer your consulting services. You should follow up your mailing with a phone call a week or two after posting your package. Ask if your mailing was received and answer any questions your recipient may have. If your contact has not seen your package, ask for a name and department and sent him one. After a while, call him again. Impress upon any potential client that you would appreciate any time he could spare for a brief meeting. The quality of your mailing is very important, and you should seriously consider having the brochure professionally typeset and printed. Your credentials as a consultant should be prominently displayed; and pictures, charts and imaginative layout can be very effective. Although putting together a mailing can be expensive, if the quality of the piece wins over just one client, the brochure will more than pay for itself. Brochures, advertisements, business cards and resumés should all be very professional. They are business expenses and can be deducted from your income tax, thereby returning some of the investment.

THE WRAP UP

This chapter reports what I have learned through my own experience as a moonlighting consultant. It's the most wide-open area among moonlighting options I have discussed so far. It is demanding, and you'll have to learn to think on your feet, and to analyze a large amount of information and juggle a number of priorities in order to come up with a single, final recommendation for your client. Consulting is a part-time career that requires confidence in your own judgment and skills. If you feel you're qualified to give it a try, and you have the tenacity and imagination to get your first few jobs, you could well be on your way to becoming a multitalented and respected moonlighting computer consultant.

SAMPLE CONSULTANT PROPOSAL

December 1, 1984

Mr. John User
ABC Manufacturing Co.
1231 Broad Street
Southampton

Dear Mr. User:

I appreciated the time you spent with me recently in reviewing your company's personal computer plans. As we discussed, I think you will see significant benefits if you install a computer to initially handle your accounts receivables and at a later date to install other applications such as order entry, invoicing and general ledger. Having performed similar studies in the past, I feel well qualified to conduct a detailed review of your data processing requirements and make recommendations as to the best approach for your company.

OBJECTIVES
The broad objective of the proposed study is an assessment of the benefits to be gained by the ABC Manufacturing Company in the installation of a personal computer.

Specifically, the goals will be to:

1. Review and comment on your present accounting operation and make suggested changes prior to putting it on a computer.

2. Assess your staff and their ability to implement and operate a computer-based accounting system.

3. Recommend a hardware configuration to initially operate the accounts receivable system, allowing for later expansion with other recommended systems.

4. Review the accounting program packages available and determine their suitability for your operation and make recommendations as to the purchase or development of such software.

5. Prepare cost estimates for the hardware and software.

6. Prepare an installation schedule.

COST AND DURATION

For the work outlined above I propose you allocate a budget for professional services of £1500. I can begin this work within three weeks of your signing this proposal. I estimate I could present my findings to you orally within one month of the beginning of the study and a written report will follow that by two weeks.

GENERAL PROVISIONS

To protect your interests I agree that any confidential information you have furnished to me during this study will be safeguarded.

This study will be done to the best of my ability and will conform with the generally accepted standards for studies of this type. I cannot be held liable for any lost profits or any other consequential damages resulting from your use of the study since I will have no control over its implementation or other use after it is delivered to you.

This proposal constitutes our entire agreement and any other statements shall not be part of this agreement.

ACCEPTANCE

This proposal is made subject to acceptance within 30 days but can be extended if you advice me.

If this proposal is acceptable, please sign and return the enclosed copy as authorization for me to proceed. If you have any questions concerning the scope or nature of the work described above, please contact me and I will be pleased to clarify or modify this proposal.

Very truly yours,

John R. Consultant

Accepted for the ABC Manufacturing Co.

By _____

Date _____

CHAPTER 7

SYSTEMS HOUSES

EQUIPMENT:
PC

EXPERTISE:
In-depth knowledge of applications, hardware, software
and installation.
User training, vendor connections, debugging and system upkeep.

CLIENT CONTACT:
Survey of application area, supervision of purchase, installation of
hardware and software, training of users and system maintenance.

FEES AND INVOICING:
Individual contract, based on requirements of job,
but averaging £20 to £30 per hour.

EXTRAS:
Writing programs, modifying or expanding systems,
writing training manuals or giving seminars.

WHAT IS A SYSTEMS HOUSE?

A *systems house*, as I'm using the term here, provides for the client a total computing system—a hardware and software system tailored to individual requirements—and all the services necessary to allow the client to begin using it, including installation, training, debugging and maintenance. I will use the term *turnkey* in referring to such a system, because all the user has to do is sit down, turn a key and begin using his computer—everything else has been provided. In many ways, this area of moonlighting begins where consulting, covered in Chapter Six, ends. If you operate a systems house, you provide essentially the same services as a consultant, but with many more responsibilities. If there is no packaged software available that completely fills your client's needs (and chances are there won't be) you must modify commercially available software, or create entirely new programming. You are responsible for installation, training, testing and long-term support once the system is running. Much of the discussion about consulting is also applicable to the moonlighting area covered in this chapter, particularly in terms of the nuts-and-bolts business details, so you will want to turn to Chapter Six first. See especially the "You and Your Client" section, page 96.

Turnkey installations have been available for many years, and they have usually been provided by professional companies, installing small to medium systems, ranging from £10,000 to £50,000, including software. However, it is possible for an individual to attempt this field. But be aware that the demands on both your time and expertise are greater here than in any other area discussed in this book, and you should be confident of your abilities, both in business and in computers, before you consider entering this field. The magnitude of the jobs available in this area make competition rather fierce, and you must be ready to market yourself aggressively if you hope to succeed.

CASE HISTORIES

These case histories will illustrate how two individuals turned modest enterprises into full-blown systems houses.

ONE. A software author who had written a package for use in personnel departments met an estate agent who was looking for a program package to improve his operations. In their discussion of the personnel program and the estate agent operations, they came to the conclusion that the program could be easily modified to handle the agent's requirements. The programmer broke his program up into modules (a good idea with a complicated program) and began to modify the code and deliver the sections to the estate agent. The first module was completed in approximately one month, written on a moonlighting basis, and testing and debugging took several additional months. Over the two years that followed, the programmer wrote and tested an entire package that automated virtually all of the record keeping for small- and medium-sized estate agency firms. This moonlighter has since sold more than 100 of these £5000+ hardware and software systems.

TWO. An individual used his familiarity with his father's fuel-oil delivery business to put together a systems house package. His father

109

devoted a lot of his time and energy to personally scheduling truck deliveries and maintaining customer invoicing and accounts due. The son wrote, tested and debugged a program that was very successful at accomplishing these tasks. His advertisements in trade-association newsletters sparked enough interest to allow him to set up a moonlighting business selling the hardware and software system he devised for his father to other fuel-oil businesses. This turnkey system cost about £10,000, and additional income was earned by customizing the system for each client.

IS IT FOR YOU?

Of all the areas of moonlighting I discuss in this book, the area of systems houses requires the largest amount of time and outside resources. The special requirements needed for this type of work will be beyond the abilities of many people, for any number of reasons. Like the other opportunities outlined in this book, this area is more easily approached from a specific background of interests, experience and lifestyle. This section should help you decide if your background is likely to add or detract from your chances of success in supplying turnkey systems.

TIME

You must have a very flexible 9-to-5 job in order to realistically pursue this particular part-time career. Although the installation of a previously designed system is less taxing, the time commitment is likely to be significant. Remember that you must be forthright with your client about your part-time status in this business, especially since you will be, in some cases, on call to your client whenever unexpected difficulties with his computer network develop.

INFORMATION SYSTEMS

You should have experience and some expertise in analyzing information systems, identifying and using relevant data, and translating everyday business transactions and files into computer system requirements.

HARDWARE AND SOFTWARE

A familiarity with the currently available hardware and software is very important. While you cannot be expected to memorize every component on the market, you should be able to locate specific information quickly. An ongoing review of the PC industry and the establishment of a filing system are the two best methods to attain and utilize this familiarity.

COMPONENT EVALUATION

You should have the ability to make hardware and software selections based on your client's system requirements. This ability will encompass, by way of example, the following considerations:
- Floppy versus hard disks
- Memory size and expansion capabilities
- Dot-matrix versus letter-quality printers
- Operating speed of different hardware/software combinations
- Vendor support.

PROGRAMMING

Experience in writing programs from "scratch" is a vital part of this type of moonlighting. My discussion of software packages (Chapter Four) covers programming requirements in detail, but it should be mentioned here that the ability to use an efficient programming language is a necessity.

If your background and lifestyle seem suited for operating a moonlighting systems house, you will be interested in what sort of clients you may find yourself working for.

WHO HIRES SYSTEMS HOUSES?

A systems house operator is likely to find clients who are small businessmen who need a computer, but who want the entire process of obtaining and preparing the system to be handled outside their company. Often, they do not have the time or interest to do the research themselves, and lack the expertise to install and design a system. If they have a small staff, they often cannot afford to allow someone on staff to head such a project, especially if their operation demands something more elaborate than can be supplied with packaged programming. Some examples of turnkey users are:
- Bank trust departments
- Doctors
- Chemists
- Small manufacturers

- Dentists
- Insurance companies

If you develop a turnkey system for a particular client, your client pool can be significantly enlarged if there are other concerns with similar data-processing needs. Such businesses might include travel agents, stockbrokers, pet shops and a myriad of others. Naturally, each system will have to be custom tailored for each client.

YOU AND YOUR CLIENT

Custom-developed turnkey systems require a good deal of consulting work. You must make a thorough survey of the system inputs, processing, and outputs necessary and discuss your findings in detail with your client to ensure your analysis is correct. Once you understand the application well, you should turn to the question of software. Determine whether there are any packaged programs that meet your client's needs. If you find a commercially available program that fits the requirements, the vendor will often supply source code with the program to allow you to make modifications. If there are no applicable packaged programs available, then you must create an original program. Naturally, writing a new program will take time and drive up your client's cost, and you should discuss this with him in detail. Once the software determinations have been made, you should be able to match hardware to software and come up with a workable combination that best serves your client.

Hiring a systems house is the most expensive way for a user to acquire a computer system, since he pays not only for hardware and software, including software development in some cases, but he also pays you a fee for your expertise and judgment. The reason your client is willing to pay more to acquire computer capabilities is that he desires what you offer him: assurance and service. He desires the assurance that his system will perform to his specifications, and that you will continue to work with the system until it does. And he desires the after-sales service that you offer: he wants to contact someone who knows the system intimately when there are problems, and that someone is you. Your client will look to you first for answers to all his computer questions, and he expects your best efforts in getting those answers for him. The assurance and service you provide would be impossible if he put the system together himself, or relied on the advice of an amateur.

In systems house work, you will develop close ties with your client. Throughout the initial development phase, the installation and the ongoing operation of your system, you will become familiar with him, his people and his business. If all goes well, a long-term relationship will be established that will benefit both of you; he will receive service and expert advice; you will earn a steady second income and valuable professional references.

FEES

The determination of your fee will probably involve three different sorts of services: consulting, the initial phase; programming charges, applicable when you write original software; and ongoing maintenance, on a retainer basis, or per call, usually after an initial period of free visits, limited to one or two months. Since every situation will differ, you must make an arrangement for each client.

As a rule, you will not make any money on the purchase of hardware or commercial software. Your client will purchase the equipment you recommend. You may recommend a retailer you've had good experience with, or accompany him to the computer store, but the actual transaction should be between your client and the retailer. Strongly recommend that your client obtain a hardware maintenance contract from the vendor, as you should not involve yourself in hardware maintenance. Of course, software problems *are* your responsibility, particularly if you wrote the software.

In an application where you provide consulting services and install a hardware/software system, your fees will probably be the baseline figure for this sort of work. Without software, such a job would generally be assessed at between £350 and £700. With software, your fee could be as high as £3500, and possibly more, depending on the complexity of the programming you write.

If you have developed a standard turnkey system for a particular application, your consulting work is likely to be minimal. In this case, it is possible that you would involve yourself with the purchase of equipment; however, this requires you take extra care to avoid overextending your finances, and it is considerably more complicated. A standard turnkey design fee is based on your work as a designer, programmer and handler of the purchases, and should run from 10% to 20% of the system cost.

MARKETING

Marketing turnkey systems, like marketing anything else, is partly a matter of playing the percentages. The more avenues you explore, the more contacts you make; the more advertising you do, the greater your chances of success.

The market for systems houses can be divided into two distinct types of enterprises: you can provide a turnkey operation tailored specifically to the individual client; or, you can design a prepackaged system for an industry application with sufficiently standard computer needs. Prepackaged systems, as mentioned earlier, often develop from a system you design for a particular client, such as the example of the fuel-oil delivery system. If you do market a system developed under contract, you will almost certainly have to arrive at some sort of marketing agreement with the original client to allow you to sell it to others in the same industry.

If you are trying to sell a systems house service of the first type, the custom-developed system, you should employ a shotgun approach, making your service known to as many people as possible who may have a potential need. Marketing a package of hardware and software that fills a specific need in a number of different fields, such as an accounts package, is known as *horizontal marketing*, and resembles in some ways the sort of marketing outlined for the consulting field in Chapter Six.

On the other hand, the process is much simpler if you can approach a vertical market by supplying a specific system to a single industry. In this case, advertising in trade journals and through direct mail, or relying on word-of-mouth are particularly effective, as are trade show appearances.

Some of the most promising ways for spreading the word on your systems house include:

ADVERTISING. Magazines, periodicals and newspapers are excellent forums for your advertisements. Special sections for professional services are available in many computer magazines and some newspapers. You might also want to investigate buying advertising time on local radio.

WORD OF MOUTH. You should always be prepared to give out your business card if the opportunity presents itself. Even if the person receiving your card is not interested in your services, it sometimes happens that someone will mention a need for your services, and your card will be passed on. Probably the best sources of leads are referrals from your clients. Do not be shy about asking your customers for the names of people who might be interested in your services.

FREELANCE WRITING. If you have had any experiences that highlight your expertise, writing for magazines is an excellent way to promote yourself in a professional manner, particularly if you describe a unique system or service that you offer. This sort of marketing is discussed in detail in Chapter Two, Freelance Writing. **RETAIL OUTLETS.** If you associate yourself with local computer stores, and make the availability of your services known, it is likely that at least a few of their customers with special applications problems will be interested in contacting you.

Running a systems house often flows naturally from a moonlighter's consulting enterprises. If you have worked as a consultant, or would like to know how some of the techniques used most profitably for consulting might be adapted to fit the needs of marketing a systems house, you may want to turn to the section entitled "Marketing Yourself", found on page 103 in Chapter Six, Consulting.

SPECIAL PROBLEMS AND OPPORTUNITIES

The largest problem in running a systems house is scheduling the large blocks of time necessary to provide adequate service. Marketing, installing and servicing an entire operations system is very demanding, and if you do not have the flexibility to provide this time, you would be best advised to choose another area of moonlighting. In addition to the consulting required in most cases, you must also be available, usually during business hours, to work with your client's staff and solve any problems that may occur.

Because of the extensive nature of the services a systems house provides, you will find that you are in competition with fulltime companies providing the same service. You will be in competition with other systems houses and with businesses that have chosen to market internally developed hardware/software systems to others in their field. In fact, some of these marketing efforts have been so successful that companies previously unconnected to the computer business have established separate groups just to handle the business they have generated.

Since you are responsible for the correction of any system malfunctions, you must be prepared to act as an efficient computer diagnostician. There are no hard-and-fast rules in diagnosing system malfunctions, but there are some hints that may save you time. Hardware failure, on the whole, is rather rare, and when it does occur, it is usually obvious, so look for software bugs and operator errors first. In a new installation, the first place to check is for operator error. Work through the procedure that caused the problem step-by-step with the operator who discovered the problem. It is very likely that you will spot an operator error if you reconstruct as precisely as possible what was happening at the time the problem manifested itself. Diagnosing software bugs is often tricky, and requires careful analysis of how the program was processing data at any particular time. Using the same data and procedures that caused the problem is very helpful.

Although the moonlighter does not have much opportunity at present to reap the benefits of a wholesaler, it is possible that discounts will be available to part-time operators in some circumstances. Some hardware vendors have recognized the sales contributions made by fulltime systems houses by instituting special programs.

Perhaps the most enticing special opportunity afforded the operator of a moonlighting turnkey service is the chance to develop a single, popular hardware/software system specially designed to meet the needs of a specific application. These prepackaged systems can be sold over and over again; the initial effort of designing the package and writing the software is soon forgotten. The moonlighter who develops a powerful system and positions himself wisely in the market could make a considerable amount of money running a very manageable part-time business.

WARRANTIES

Warranties for the system you install should be approached carefully. Hardware warranties should concern your client and the manufacturer and not you. As far as the entire system is concerned, you should limit your obligations to warranting that the system will perform according to your established specifications, as long as the system is unaltered and correctly operated. In the case of a custom-designed system, the specifications you guarantee are those you and your client agreed to at the outset. At the least, they should cover the volume of data the system can handle, the type and format of the input data, and the reports available from the system.

You must always include a section in your warranty that excludes all liability on your part for any consequential or incidental losses or damages, including losses of income or unrealized savings through the use of, or inability to use, the system.

THE FUTURE

There will continue to be a market for systems house services, but it is my opinion that it will not grow as quickly as the overall PC market. More and more software packages are being written for specialized applications, and the programs are becoming easier for those with little or no experience to use. In the next ten or fifteen years, systems will become simpler to assemble and maintain, and the chances of unexpected problems that may require professional assistance will decrease. The steady decline in hardware costs may also make it increasingly difficult to justify the expense of hiring someone to put the system together, just as the steady deployment of computer knowledge will reduce this need.

There will always be people who want a computer system but are not willing to find out about computers, and are, therefore, willing to pay someone to perform the task. The service and assurance offered by the moonlighting systems house operator will always find a market, but you should be aware that market forces in the next few years will eliminate many of the least talented and least qualified providers of turnkey systems.

BUSINESS CONSIDERATIONS

The advice and analysis in this chapter is presented for informational purposes only and does not attempt to provide legal or accounting advice. Business, tax and other regulations are subject to change, and you should investigate current regulations for yourself. Legal, accounting and other professional services and guidance should be obtained only from properly qualified sources.

YOUR NEW BUSINESS

The scope and complexity of a personal computer moonlighting enterprise can range from something little more demanding than a hobby to a full-blown and very time-consuming small business. Your business can be as demanding as your time and interest allow. In the majority of cases, your second career will not involve very much in the way of business organization and paperwork; the extent of your extra responsibilities may be a slightly more complicated income tax return once a year. For the most part, your business considerations will be affected by the amount of money you take in for any given year—if you do not make more than a few hundred pounds from your secondary income, things should be fairly simple. However, if you feel there is some chance that your moonlighting activities may one day replace your present job, the establishment of good business practices at the outset will greatly ease that transformation. This chapter will set forth most of the basic skills and knowledge that you will need to run a successful small business in your spare time.

RECORD KEEPING

One of the most frequent causes of business failure is inadequate record keeping. Poor record-keeping practices force you to operate in the dark much of the time. If you do not know where you have been, you will have a hard time determining where you should go. The informed businessman uses accurate records of his activities to identify potential problems before they manifest themselves. Good records are necessary to substantiate your tax returns, to provide data to potential investors, and to establish credit with your suppliers. Keep in mind that your PC is an excellent tool for keeping business record in line, as well as for evaluating the effects of different strategies and business practices. Your "books" should be easy to use, up-to-date and accurate. At the very least, they should provide the answers to the following questions:

- What is my gross income?
- What are my expenses, and do they seem in line?
- What is my profit margin?
- How much cash do I have on hand?
- What are my other assets?
- How much do I owe (accounts payable)?
- How much is owed me (accounts receivable)?
- How does each separate job break down in terms of income, outgoings and invoicing?
- What are the trends in sales, profits and assets?
- What is my current tax liability?

There are two basic methods of keeping accounting records, they are:

- Single entry bookkeeping
- Double entry bookkeeping

For the beginning moonlighter, or an established moonlighter running a medium-sized business, I think that single-entry book-keeping is the best method. Your record-keeping chores will be kept to a minimum and the information should be more than enough to allow you to run your business well. For any transaction, only one entry is made, either to income or expenses. Whereas this will provide the needed records, it will not give you bookkeeping information such as inventory levels, nor will it provide complete information about total assets and liabilities at a glance. It also lacks the checks and balances of the double-entry method, so you will have to be careful to record all data accurately. For tax purposes, the system records the flow of income and expenses through the use of a daily summary or cash receipts, a monthly summary of receipts and a monthly summary of disbursements. Whilst it is possible to submit figures to the Inland Revenue without consulting an accountant,

119

because of the complexities of the Income Tax Acts it is as well to do so. Fees are on a time basis and much of the costs can be recouped by advice on tax avoidance. He will advise you on the best bookkeeping system. Any good business stationers will carry the necessary forms and ledgers for both single- and double-entry bookkeeping systems.

Unless your brother-in-law is an accountant, I would suggest avoiding the double-entry system until the complexity of your business demands it. Assuming that you are a sole proprietor (see below), the single-entry sysem will serve your needs quite well. The double-entry method requires two entries for each transaction, one a debit and the other a credit. For instance, if you buy a desk, your cash account would receive a credit, while your furniture and fixtures account would see a debit. The double-entry method provides a very detailed record of the movement of capital into, out of and within your business. As each transaction is made, it is entered into a journal, which is a day-to-day record of your operations; then, usually on a monthly basis, summary totals are entered into ledgers. Ledger accounts are usually of five types: income, expenses, assets, liabilities and net worth. Since every transaction is entered as a credit and a debit, the system is self-balancing, and you can easily match up credits and debits to make sure that you have done everything right. While double-entry accounting provides much more detailed information, its additional complexity rarely makes it preferable to the single-entry method. If your business is a partnership, you may want to consider double-entry, and you should certainly consider it if you choose to incorporate. The sole proprietor, owner of the most common form of moonlighting business organization, should generally confine his record keeping to single-entry bookkeeping.

BUSINESS ORGANIZATION

Once you have decided to go into business for yourself, you must decide how you want to organize your operation. The choice of your organizational form affects the amount of paperwork to which you are subjected, the ease with which you can raise capital, obtain credit and expand your business, your start-up costs, your tax situation, and your legal liability. There are three basic forms of business organization:

- Sole proprietorship
- Partnership
- Corporation

SOLE PROPRIETORSHIP

The majority of small businesses are sole proprietorships. This is the simplest form of business organization, and I would suggest that all moonlighters begin simply. A sole proprietorship comes into existence when an individual starts to do business. It is by far the easiest business to start up, and at the most, you may have to comply with the Companies Acts and register the trading name of your business if you decide not to trade in your own name. A business organized this way has only one owner—you—and has no existence apart from you. If you die, your business dies with you.

A sole proprietorship business is not deemed to be a separate legal entity; its profits or losses are part of your personal income and the taxes it pays are part of your individual tax liabilities and as such must be declared in the relevant section of your personal tax return. For Income Tax purposes the sole proprietorship's tax liability is assessed under Schedule D cases I or II 'Profits arising from a Trade (Case I) or Profession of Vocation (Case II)', and are assessed on the profits made by the business based on an annual Profit and Loss account. Certain expenses of a business which are incurred, may, however, not be allowable for income tax purposes and the profit per the accounts may have to be adjusted.

The income tax year runs to the 5th April but the annual accounts need not run to that date. The normal basis for assessment under Schedule D Cases I and II is the profits of the accounts year ending in the preceding tax year. Thus if a busines makes up its accounts to 31st December the 1984–85 assessment would be based on the profits to 31st December, 1983 (i.e. ending in the previous tax year 1983–84). If your business makes a loss you may set the loss against other sources of income in the same tax year or carry the loss forward to set against future profits.

The only real disadvantage to the sole proprietorship is that its legal liabilities become your personal liabilities. Because the sole proprietorship has no existence apart from you, all your personal assets are at risk. If you are sued, your home, car and all other assets could be in danger. It is unlikely that, as a moonlighter, you will become embroiled in a serious lawsuit, but the possibility does, of course, exist. In the more involved areas of moonlighting, you can minimize these risks by careful attention to contracts and warranties. It is also possible, in some cases, to take out insurance against the

121

risks of unlimited liability. Generally referred to as "Errors and Omissions Insurance" (E & O), it is analogous to medical malpractice insurance. However, it may be difficult and expensive for an individual to obtain this kind of insurance, so you should carefully consider the cost and the extent of your potential liability before you make any decisions about insurance.

PARTNERSHIP

A partnership is a legal relationship existing between two or more persons who jointly manage a trade or business. A partnership is established through an agreement, usually written, called a *partnership agreement*. Each partner contributes money, labour, property or skill to the business, and agrees to share in its profits or losses. In its simplest form, the partners go fifty-fifty, but other breakdowns are possible. A general partner takes an active part in running the business, while a limited partner generally functions as an investor, with no voice in the operations of the enterprise. Limited partnerships are summarized later in this section.

A partnership is essentially a sole proprietorship run by more than one person. Like the sole proprietorship, a partnership is legally indistinguishable from the people who run it—each partner figures the business' profit or loss on his personal tax return. Like the sole proprietorship, the partnership is also quite simple to set up. A handshake and a verbal agreement are all that are legally required to start doing business, though a written agreement is very strongly recommended. Your partnership agreement should include, at the very least, the following stipulations:

- A statement of the partnership's goals and objectives.
- The contributions each partner will make in terms of time, money, and property.
- Whether and at what percentage interest is to be paid on the capital introduced.
- How the partners will share the profit or loss.
- Procedures for the withdrawal of funds and distribution of profits.
- A contingency plan covering the voluntary withdrawal or death of a partner.

Just as the partners are legally indistinguishable from their business, so they are indistinguishable from each other. Each partner is jointly and severally liable for the debts and obligations of the business, and one partner can legally commit the entire partnership in any agreement or transaction. Legal liability incurred by one partner, including any fraudulent or other illegal activity, flows directly to the other partner.

Although a partnership is a more involved way for a moonlighter to form a business, the potential advantages of pooling talents, skills and capital are often great. By joining forces, a technician and a businessman can accomplish more than either can alone, and the addition of a financier can greatly ease the problems of starting your own business on a shoestring budget. Another type of partnership involves a limited partner. For the limited partner, the business organization provides some of the liability protection of the corporation. Limited partners, for the most part, are investors that have no say in how the business is operated. (For this reason, they are sometimes referred to as "silent partners".) A partnership, however, must have at least one general partner. As long as a limited partner is not involved in running the business, his personal assets are not at risk, as are the assets of the general partners. A limited partner cannot lose anything more than the monies he has invested. For this reason, limited partners can occasionally be of great help to the moonlighter who needs to raise start-up and operating capital. However, limited partnerships are subject to far greater governmental scrutiny than the general partnership, primarily because of the complicated tax situation of the limited partner, and for this reason, expert professional advice, ideally provided by a lawyer, is strongly recommended.

CORPORATION

It is unlikely that the PC moonlighter will ever be in a position to start a corporation. Incorporation is a very big step, and brings with it an enormous amount of additional paperwork, operational and legal requirements. In nearly all cases, the moonlighter should consider incorporating *if* he wishes to transform his part-time activities into a fulltime business, and even then, the corporation may be more trouble than it is worth.

A corporation, unlike the other two organizational forms covered, is considered a *bona fide* legal entity, with an existence separate from the people associated with it. For this reason, the primary differences of a corporation are found in the areas of taxes and liability.

A corporation is owned by one or more shareholders, making it easier to add or remove investors or shareholders. Thus, the continuity of a corporation is insured, even if a shareholder dies or chooses to leave the business. For many reasons, some psychological and some practical, other corporations and banks often prefer to deal with corporations. If your business is incorporated, rather than organized as a sole proprietorship or partnership, it will usually be easier to obtain credit or a loan.

Probably the major reason to consider incorporating, though, is the limited personal liability afforded the owners (shareholders). If a corporation either cannot pay its debts, or is sued, personal assets are not placed at risk. This is called *limited liability* because doing business deceitfully or perpetrating fraud still makes you vulnerable to a personal lawsuit and negates your protection. Also, in many cases, companies will not do business with a small corporation unless its owners accept personal liability. The liability protection afforded by incorporation, though not complete, does offer considerably more protection than either a sole proprietorship or a partnership.

A corporation is a taxable entity, with tax rates ranging as high as 52%. Playing the corporate tax game can become enormously complicated and involuted, and expert guidance is strongly recommended. However, there are some guidelines to keep in mind, and these are outlined below.

RETENTION OF EARNINGS. Corporations can carry cash and other liquid assets over from year to year, but they must pay a tax on these retained earnings. Corporate profits distributed to employees or shareholders in the form of wages, dividends or bonuses are also subject to personal income tax, essentially a second tax. (Corporation tax is the first tax.) But, if shareholders are considered employees, distributed profits can be considered wages, which can be deducted by the corporation as a business expense as opposed to a dividend, which cannot. Be aware, though, that the Inland Revenue looks carefully at such payments to shareholders/employees to determine whether they should properly be considered wages or dividends.

LOSSES. One tax disadvantage of the corporation is the treatment of losses. In the other two business forms, if the company loses money in a particular year, the loss can be subtracted from the owners' income for that year in computing personal income tax. Corporate losses, however, must be applied to the profits for other years.

PAPERWORK. The paperwork required to set up a corporation and keep it running is very demanding. You must establish a board of directors, which must have meetings and keep minutes, keep many financial records, and file a complicated Corporation Tax Return CTI(Z).

Again, I would strongly advise the moonlighter to begin business as a sole proprietor. It will get your business going more quickly and with fewer headaches. As your business progresses and expands, you may want to eventually consider partnership and, possibly, incorporation.

TAX CONSIDERATIONS FOR MOONLIGHTERS

This section provides some of the basic facets of tax liability as they apply to the PC moonlighter. You can find out much more from a variety of publications issued by the Inland Revenue, one of the most helpful being *Starting in Business* (IR28) and you may want to get some general business advice from your local chamber of commerce. If you find that your taxes are somewhat complicated at the end of the year, you should seriously consider having them prepared by an accountant. Often, the money spent for this service is offset by the reduction in your tax liabilities.

TAX SCHEDULE D. As a sole proprietor operating your own business, you are entitled to the same tax considerations as any other commercial enterprise, including such expenditures as advertising, bad debts, association and club dues, publications and other research expenses, legal and other professional services, repairs, rent and equipment, office supplies, and postage. Section 130 of the Income and Corporation Taxes Act 1970 details expenses *not* deductable from business profits.

Tax schedule D can only be used if your enterprise is deemed to be operating for profit. According to the Inland Revenue, if an activity results in a profit for two or more years in any successive five years, it is presumed to have been operating for profit. If it did not, and you cannot show otherwise, the IR will presume your activity to be a hobby. The primary difference between a hobby and a business operated for profit is that a hobby cannot declare a loss. If your business has gone five years without a profit, advertising expenses, business cards and stationery, and an accounting system may help you convince the IR that you are operating a business, not a hobby.

CAPITAL ALLOWANCES. Expenditure on your PC and furniture used exclusively for the business will be subject to a Capital Allowance. This will either take the form of a first year allowance in which the whole of the purchase price is allowable against your assessed profit in the year of purchase; or a writing down allowance over the life of the assets. When selling or trading in your PC you may be subjected to a Balancing Charge or Allowance which is the difference between the written down value and the sale proceeds. Capital Allowances are deducted from your assessable profits or may augment a loss.

USE OF YOUR HOME FOR BUSINESS. The Inland Revenue has very specific guidelines for charging expenses of your home against your business profits. Home expenses such as telephone are allowable after deducting the private proportion. For most of the other expenses such as heat and light, rates and mortgage repayments, the business share is difficult to determine. The Inland Revenue will allow a nominal sum; if you charge more, by justifying the extra allowance you may find when selling your home that you have lost your Capital Gains Tax exemption on the business proportion. In addition, you may find that your business proportion of the house may be commercially rated by your Local Council which is more expensive.

VALUE ADDED TAX. Until such times as your turnover exceeds a certain sum (£18,000 or £6000 in a calendar quarter from March 1983) you need not register for VAT. As soon as it does you must inform the Customs & Excise who will register you. Not being registered means you cannot claim back VAT suffered on your expenses but you do not have to charge your customers an extra 15%. Being registered means each quarter you must fill in a return recording details of turnover, VAT suffered and collected, and pay the balance to the Customs & Excise. At this juncture your bookkeeping will have to be more sophisticated.

NATIONAL INSURANCE CONTRIBUTIONS. Even though you may have had N.I. Contributions deducted from your fulltime salary you must still purchase a weekly Class 2 self-employed National Insurance stamp (1983–84 £4.40). You will also be subjected to a charge of 6.3% (1983–84) on your taxable profits in excess of £3800. Your contributions are, however, aggregated and you may be due for a refund from the Department of Health and Social Security.

ESTIMATED TAX ASSESSMENTS. The Inspector of Taxes

may well estimate your income from your moonlighting activities. This is little more than a guess as to profits and is usually raised when your accounts are outstanding. You must appeal against the estimate within 30 days and ask to have the tax payable postponed or reduced.

OTHER COMPUTER DEDUCTIONS

If you are not an established moonlighting business, there are still ways you can deduct the costs of PCs from your income tax.

• The Inland Revenue may allow you to deduct a proportion of the cost of your PC from your taxable income if it is required for the performance of your fulltime job. If you can show that your computer allows you to maintain and improve the job skills required by your employer, or that the use of the computer is necessary to meet express requirements for keeping your job, you may be able to deduct its costs. In cases like this, it is a good idea to have a letter from your employer, or a copy of any regulations that substantiate your claim.

• If your moonlighting activities are defined as a hobby, rather than a business for profit, you may deduct the costs, including interest and operating expenses up to the amount of your hobby income. As mentioned earlier, you may not declare a loss from a hobby.

• If your computer can be demonstrated as necessary to prepare your tax returns, manage investments, or maintain records of property held for income, you may deduct a proportion of its costs from your taxable income.

CONTRACTS

Several sections of this book discuss work that is done under contract, and the content of these contracts. Although it is beyond the scope of this book to define all the possible permutations of moonlighting contracts, the next best thing is a general outline that can be added to or modified for specific moonlighting situations. The most important rule is *write it down* (if at all possible), never rely on a verbal agreement. Any contract you sign should cover the following points:

• A summary of the purpose of the contract.
• A detailed summary of the responsibilities of each party.
• Payment terms, and the schedule of payments.

- When the work is to be delivered, or the job completed
- Actions to be taken on the default of either party.

GOOD LUCK

Computer moonlighters may find themselves doing hundreds of different kinds of work, in as many different business contexts. I cannot cover everything that might come up, nor can I protect you from all the risks of doing business as an independent. What I have included in this section should be regarded only as the skeleton, or perhaps, several alternative skeletons, on which you can build your business. Learn from those who have preceded you; talk about the mistakes they made, and the things that pulled them out of difficult spots. There are a lot of moonlighters out there, and for the most part, they are willing to help each other out, at least with good advice. Watch your step, and make sure you don't get in over your head. If you have never run a business before, you should not be too nervous about starting one; what is most needed in business is common sense, and the ability to stay on top of things. If you have run a business before, the broad outlines will be familiar, but you will discover that, in many ways, the computer business lives by rules peculiar to itself: allow yourself time to learn the territory. Good luck to all moonlighters, amateur and seasoned businessman alike: I hope everything works out for the best.

LAST WORDS

What I have tried to present in this book is an overview of the personal computer field as it stands today and an outline of the areas I believe can be profitably entered by the moonlighting computer operator. You will face the same opportunities, and the same obstacles, in starting up a moonlighting operation that you would encounter in establishing any small business. There are no ten easy steps you can follow to guarantee your success. But the PC industry is booming and, though it has been said before, the ground floor really *is* open to you.

As I mentioned at the very beginning of the book, the secret to all this, if there is any secret at all, is to determine where the needs lie and put yourself in a position to fill one. Moonlighting with your personal computer is a matter of being in the right place at the right time. The right time for many of the opportunities I have sketched for you is right now. And there are hundreds of right places for you to set out toward. Some of the things I've talked about you could start right away, without much more knowledge or equipment than you have right now. Some of the more demanding areas require you to have either special equipment, or a body of specialized expertise. If you have the equipment and knowledge now, you are one jump ahead of many of your potential competitors. If you do not, a dedicated effort to gain what you lack could be accomplished more easily than you might suspect, for this a field where only a few years separate the seasoned professional from the rank amateur. If you get "on the ball" quickly, any head start you are working against can be made up close to the starting line.

Although I divided my topics from one another in discussing them, for clarity's sake, it is important to realize that the lines between areas are not so rigidly drawn. Many of the areas I've talked about can be entered most easily from one of the other areas. Activity in the personal computer field tends to flow naturally between endeavours that might seem at first glance to be distant from one another. You may view moonlighting as a simple addition to your income, the opportunity to develop one particular product and sell it. But the field, at the moment, seems to attract more than its fair share of entrepreneurs, individuals who learn the turf quickly, and readily move on to areas yet to be exploited, or to segments of the market with a high concentration of activity at any given moment. It is from the pool of entrepreneurs that the new crop of computer millionaires will spring; indeed, for a lucky few, that first million is already in the bank. The PC world is young and full of vitality. Cross fertilization is becoming one of the most important mechanisms of new growth, and, if you are the adventurous sort, penetrating the unexplored jungles of this new world may well be one of the last truly romantic ventures left for you. A very attractive feature of the moonlighting option is, of course, that you are insulated from the most frightening risks of dropping everything and setting out in a new direction. You can test the waters, and if they seem hospitable, you can go a little further. You may find yourself at some point leaving your fulltime job for the career you have established in moonlighting.

If none of the ideas I've covered appeal to you, and you are not sure which PC areas you would like to explore, try this: make a list of the various sorts of products and services you would feel comfortable and confident supplying, even if they seem obvious or silly. One of the mistakes many people make when they attempt exercises like this is assuming that an idea or product seems so obvious, that someone must have already thought of it; often, just because the field is so new, no one has, or if they have, it is still not on the market. The more you force yourself into this brainstorming method for generating new ideas, the more sensible and workable these ideas will become, until you hit on one that really grabs you. When you come up with an idea that really gets you excited, *that* is the one to try.

I cannot overemphasize the importance of developing techniques to keep yourself abreast of new developments in this fast-moving field. One of the best ways to keep up is to regularly read several of the personal computing magazines now available, and to supplement your reading with regular visits to PC exhibits and shows, and membership in a PC club. The exchange of ideas with your computing peers is one of the best ways to keep your business flexible and growing (some PC magazines list these clubs for all areas of the country).

A realistic evaluation of yourself, in terms of those qualities likely to aid the establishment of a business, can help you immeasurably in making the basic decisions that will dictate the parameters of your moonlighting endeavours. Although tests such as the one pointed here must be taken with a grain of salt, filling out this inventory can be a valuable way to start you thinking realistically about yourself as an independent businessperson. Give it a try. If you have been honest in your self-evaluation, and most of your answers cluster on the left side of the scale, you have the personality this test is looking for. If more are on the right side, you may need a partner to help fill in those areas in which you are weakest. If you bring in someone else, though do not forget to set down your terms in writing.

One way to decide where to start is knowing which areas are the easiest to enter. Though this will vary enormously from person to person, depending on background, talent, and perseverance, I have discussed the areas roughly in order of increasing entrance difficulty. Here is a summary.

FREELANCE WRITING. This is generally the easiest because you have a tangible product to sell, not a service, and the product you are selling can be wholly determined by your capability. Instead of competing directly with people who have much more computer expertise, you can simply seek out markets that are interested in publishing what it is you know. If you really work at it, you can almost certainly sell an article to someone. In-depth technical knowledge is not required of freelance writers, but you do have to be conscious of deadlines. Because there is little end–user contact, your work proceeds the way you decide it should.

SERVICE BUREAU. Although there is the responsibility of handling your customer's work directly, service bureaux can be started with almost no technical knowledge, if you use packaged software. If you wish, running a service bureau can be as simple as routine office work after a little practice, although service bureaux do offer considerable opportunity to expand in step with your increasing ability. The most demanding aspects of service-bureau work is likely to be handling the logistics of it—scheduling delivery, processing and return of the work—and taking the extra care necessary to ensure accuracy and provide back-up files.

PACKAGED PROGRAMS. Because you have a tangible product

to demonstrate to potential buyers, your marketing task is considerably simpler than in the remaining moonlighting areas. There are many established distribution companies to sell your programs through, and self-marketing, in some cases, is a promising alternative. But this area does demand a considerable level of technical skill, if you are to produce marketable software. The ability to write code and prepare adequate documentation, while it comes more naturally to some than others, is not achieved by anyone without a large investment of time and energy.

CONTRACT PROGRAMMING. This is the first area that requires you to encounter professional businessmen face-to-face. For moonlighters already in business, or those with a number of business contacts, this area is a natural way to profitably sell your programming ability. For those who have never braved the waters of real-life business, you will have to learn the ropes while you learn to sell your programming skills. Direct client contact, the need to work within deadlines comfortably, and the necessity of developing a marketable level of expertise in a particular application area or programming language, makes this a rather demanding moonlighting option. However, the contract programmer does have the advantage of working primarily on his own time and, in the end, delivering a product that usually requires a minimum amount of after-the-sale effort.

RATING SCALE FOR PERSONAL TRAITS
IMPORTANT TO A BUSINESS PROPRIETOR

After each question place a tick on the line at the point closest to your answer. The tick need not be placed directly over one of of the suggested answers because your rating may lie somewhere between two answers. Be honest with yourself.

_____ ARE YOU A SELF STARTER? _____

| I do things my own way. Nobody needs to tell me to get going. | If someone gets me started, I keep going all right. | Easy does it. I don't put myself out until I have to. |

_____ HOW DO YOU FEEL ABOUT OTHER PEOPLE? _____

| I like people. I can get along with just about anybody. | I have plenty of friends. I don't need anyone else. | Most people irritate me. |

CAN YOU LEAD OTHERS?

I can get most people to go along without much difficulty.

I can get people to do things if I drive them.

I let someone else get things moving.

CAN YOU TAKE RESPONSIBILITY?

I like to take charge and see things through.

I'll take over if I have to, but I'd rather let someone else be responsible.

There's always some eager beaver around wanting to show off. I say let him.

HOW GOOD AN ORGANIZER ARE YOU?

I like to have a plan before I start. I'm usually the one to get things lined up.

I do all right unless things get too mixed up. Then I cop out.

I just take things as they come.

HOW GOOD A WORKER ARE YOU?

I can keep going as long as necessary. I don't mind working hard.

I'll work hard for a while, but when I've had enough, that's it!

I can't see that hard work gets you anywhere.

CAN YOU MAKE DECISIONS?

I can make up my mind in a hurry if necessary, and my decision is usually o.k.

I can if I have plenty of time. If I have to make up my mind fast, I usually regret it.

I don't like to be the one who decides things. I'd probably mess it up.

CAN PEOPLE TRUST WHAT YOU SAY?

Yes. I don't say things I don't mean.

I try to be on the level, but sometimes I just say what's easiest.

What's the problem if the other person doesn't know the difference?

CAN YOU STICK WITH IT?

If I make up my mind to do something, I don't let anything stop me.

I usually finish what I start.

If a job doesn't go right, I turn off. Why beat your brains out?

HOW GOOD IS YOUR HEALTH?

I never get run down.

I have enough energy for most things I want to do.

I run out of juice sooner than most of my friends seem to.

133

CONSULTING. Instead of marketing a tangible product, the consultant sells his judgment and expertise alone. Establishing a reputation as a consultant is demanding even for expert computer users. It takes time, patience and a spotless track record to achieve a stable presence in the consulting market. Consulting also requires an in-depth knowledge of computer applications across the board if you are to provide real service to your client. However, the PC field is so new that no one, except some that have worked with large computer systems, has more than a few years of useful expertise.

SYSTEMS HOUSES. Not only does this area require an extensive background of technical computer ability, often including the creation of custom-designed software, but the time required to properly develop and maintain this type of business demands the moonlighter organize his time and activities to the smallest detail. The most comfortable way to run a systems house on a moonlighting basis is to design a system that can be sold with minor modification to a large number of clients.

It is estimated that about 1.8 million PCs were sold in the UK in 1983. The estimate for 1984 is three million. After that, it is anybody's guess. The trend in personal computing is more for less. The speed and capabilities of hardware will increase as the price comes down. Software will become ever more friendly, easy to use and forgiving, and the prices will drop, though not as quickly as will the prices for hardware. Program creation is labour intensive, and highly trained people don't come cheap.

Although my crystal ball gets a little cloudy if I look more than one or two years into the future, there is little doubt that moonlighting opportunities will soon be most plentiful in the software packaging industry. The PC will attract more and more people who will know less and less about computers, so powerful, user-friendly software will be more and more in demand. Freelance writing as a field will also continue to expand, simply as a way to provide all these newcomers with the know-how and techniques that they will be demanding. As the use of PCs expands, and the proliferation of products becomes increasingly confusing, small business, left behind momentarily by the computer revolution, will ensure a strong market for consultants and those running systems houses.

Most people do not purchase PCs simply to jump on the latest technology bandwagon, but because a computer can solve a particular problem for them better than anything else can. Hardware, software and related products are only specific means to particular ends. The key for the individual considering entry to the PC field is to concentrate his efforts toward providing solutions to problems.

When I began my career, computers were just entering the working world. I needed an engineering degree and a lot of specialized education to get my start. The computers I learned on were big and expensive and their secrets were known only to a relative few. Although the germ of the personal computer was contained in these monsters, only the passage of years, the work of thousands of highly trained people, and a host of technological breakthroughs could have put this computer power on your kitchen table. The technological, and hence, economic power placed in the hands of so many is unprecedented. Perhaps the personal computer may prove to be one of the most liberating, equalizing inventions the human race will invent. With almost breathtaking suddenness, an enormous new landscape is opened to all who make an effort to become a part of it. I hope this book will provide many, many people with the first, modest steps toward carving a place for themselves in the new world being ushered in right now in these, the first days of the Information Age.

APPENDIX A

PROGRAMMING LANGUAGES

A personal computer does not actually run the code that you write. Any computer language must be translated within the computer to *object code*, strings of ones and zeroes, before it can be used. Programming languages can be placed in either of two categories, interpretive or compiler, depending on how this translation is accomplished.

Although the translation job is basically the same in both compiler and interpretive languages, the difference lies in timing. Interpretive languages translate the program line by line each time it runs, while compiler languages translate the entire program once when it is compiled, and then store a complete program as object code for later runs. Some languages, like BASIC, are available in both types, allowing programs to be written and debugged in the interpretive mode, and then compiled and run as compiled object code, increasing the efficiency of the run.

Interpretive languages have certain advantages, including these:

• Immediate execution and instant error reporting.

• When a program written in an interpretive language is halted, the state of all variables and other data can be examined.

• Some interpreters will switch to a line-editing mode to allow easy error correction.

Compiler benefits include the following:

• One time translation, which generally speeds program execution.

• The compiler, as a separate program, does not reside in memory during program execution, freeing memory space that is used throughout execution by intrepretive languages for continuous translation.

• Only object code need be delivered to the end user, providing considerably more security than the delivery of source code necessary in interpretive programs.

Programming languages for PCs are constantly evolving, but some of the more popular, currently available languages include

- BASIC—both compiler and interpretive
- Pascal and Modula-2—compiler
- Assembler—compiler
- C Language—compiler
- FORTH—compiler
- FORTRAN—compiler
- LOGO—interpretive

BASIC. BASIC is the ideal language for the beginner or relatively inexperienced programmer because it is easier to learn than most, and because there is a wealth of educational material to help you learn it, including books, classroom instruction, video cassettes and diskette tutors that run on many PCs. Interpretive BASIC comes standard, in one version or another, with nearly every PC sold today, and compiler BASIC is available for many at an additional cost. A great many packaged application programs are written in some version of BASIC, making it much easier for the user to make modifications should the source code be available from the vendor. A brief survey of close to 50 payroll packages currently available for the PC found that some form of BASIC was the most common language used, and that source code was made available by about half the vendors.

PASCAL AND MODULA-2. Pascal was originally written to teach the principles of structured programming, and is probably the second most popular PC programming language. Although Pascal forces the programmer to write readable, structured code, which is an excellent habit to develop early in your programming career, it is weak in its input/output operations. This input/output weakness forces the user to use nonstandard extensions, limiting the program's portabiltiy. The developer of Pascal, Nicklaus Wirth, has recently developed a programming language called Modula-2 that is said to overcome the shortcomings of Pascal without sacrificing any of the advantages. The Volkswriter word-processing package is written in Pascal.

ASSEMBLY LANGUAGE. This language uses symbolic codes to represent machine language for the specific microprocessor chip, and is therefore considered a low-level (close to machine language) language, as opposed to the higher-level (more English-like) languages like COBOL and FORTRAN. Due to its symbolic nature,

137

Assembly Language is difficult to learn, but produces very efficient programs, particularly valuable in large systems where run times are critical. A popular database system, dBASE II, is written in Assembly Language. .

C LANGUAGE. C Language was developed at Bell Laboratories. Although it is very powerful, it is easier to learn than Assembler. Although users praise its high portability, the lack of self-documentation is considered by some to be a drawback, and the compiled code tends to be large in comparison to the source code. If your programs are simple, and intended primarily for the home market, BASIC is a good choice. But for large, complicated applications, such as a word-processing system where speed of execution is an important consideration, C Language is recommended. Adherents to this language, like those of FORTH, tend to be fanatically committed to it. Two word-processing packages, *Easywriter II* and *The Final Word*, are written in C Language.

FORTH. A highly transportable language, FORTH is unfortunately unsuitable for the novice programmer. Using FORTH requires a good deal of concentration, and a background in other programming languages. You will have to wait for all the pieces of FORTH to fit together before you will really feel comfortable with it.

FORTRAN. This is one of the oldest compiler languages. Considered a "scientific" language, as opposed to the "business" language, COBOL, FORTRAN is most useful for number crunching. Because the two languages are similar, BASIC can serve as an excellent introduction to FORTRAN.

LOGO. LOGO was originally developed to teach children the concepts of programming. It is ideal for those interested in learning a first computer language, because someone with little experience can write a working program rather quickly. Its use, however, has gone far beyond the children's level. LOGO, like BASIC, is an interpretive language, and its structure resembles PASCAL. In fact, some people recommend that LOGO be studied before moving on to PASCAL.

■■■■■■■■■■■■■■■■■■
■■■■■■■ APPENDIX B ■■■■■■■
DOCUMENTATION GUIDELINES

The quality of personal computer software is a significant factor in the acceptance of PCs by the vast majority of people; software documentation, in turn, is extremely important to the acceptance of the software itself. Documentation for applications programs and hardware systems has a reputation that ranges from good to very poor and a large part of the acceptance of what you produce as a moonlighter can hinge on the documentation you prepare to support it.

The key to preparing good software documentation is an understanding of your user and what he is looking for. What is your user's level of experience? How will he use this material? If you are writing documentation for a program you have written, keep in mind that your supporting material will be used by someone completely unfamiliar with your program. Although you have been involved in writing the code, and designing highly involved routines, your documentation is not primarily intended to explain your program, but to instruct someone in how to use it. The best way to test a draft of your documentation is to get someone unacquainted with the program to use it and give you a review. There is no substitute for this method, and omitting it can be a severe impediment to the success of your product. If you are writing documentation for an entire system, it is important that you do not settle on a final version until the system has been used for a time with your documentation; then you may evaluate the performance of your documentation based on a real-life situation.

I have developed a checklist to help you evaluate the user documentation for your programs. At a minimum, it should include the following:

- A table of contents, an index and a glossary. These reference aids should be augmented by summary lists (e.g. special codes), a bibliography and headings on each page indicating what is being covered.

- An introduction to the manual and to each chapter that explains, at the novice level, how the system operates.
- Examples that show facets of the program in actual operation.
- Trouble-shooting sections that will make the user independent, providing self-diagnosis and error-correction guides.
- Illustrations and examples that will minimize the need for extensive narrative description of specific program features. Illustrations should be labelled and keyed to the text.
- All abbreviations, acronyms and symbols should be defined the first time they are used and included in the glossary.
- Headings in the text that will help the reader scan for specific information.

When supplying modifiable program code direct to your client, or when installing a complete hardware/software system, your documentation should include the following:

- A system narrative that describes in words how the system works, and also describes the relationships between various processing modules and major files.
- A system flow diagram showing major programs and files and how data is routed through the system.
- Individual program descriptions and flow diagrams.
- Detailed file definitions.
- Editing rules for data input.
- Report writing specifications.

If you plan to make source code available to the users of your software, you should consider internal documentation—remark lines within the actual source code that explain the purpose of each subroutine and otherwise help guide the user to a working knowledge of how you have designed your program. I once heard of a programming shop, that used BASIC and required as many remark lines as programming code lines. While this may seem excessive to you, it will not be to a programmer trying to figure out how your program works. The test for good internal documentation is whether a programmer or analyst that knows the language in which you are programming can maintain the program, or make changes, using only the internal documentation you have provided.

PERSONAL COMPUTER MAGAZINES

UK, Ireland, US imports, South Africa, Australia and New Zealand.

A & B Computing,
Argus Specialist Publications Ltd,
1 Golden Square,
London, W1R 3AB

Appleuser,
Database Publications Ltd,
68 Chester Road,
Hazel Grove,
Stockport,
Greater Manchester, SK7 5NY

A–Z of Personal Computers,
Video Press,
12 Kingsbridge Avenue,
London, W3

BBC Micro User,
Database Publications,
68 Chester Road,
Hazel Grove,
Stockport,
Greater Manchester, SK7 5NY

Business Computer World,
10a Dryden Street,
London, WC2E 9NA

Byte Magazine,
McGraw Hill,
70 Main Street,
Peterborough,
New Hampshire,
NH 03458,
U.S.A.

Commodoreuser,
The Paradox Group Ltd,
The Metropolitan,
Enfield Road,
London, N1 5AZ

Computer Answers,
VNU Business Publications BV,
Evelyn House,
62 Oxford Street,
London, W1A 2HG

Computer Choice,
Electrical–Electronic Press,
Quadrant House,
The Quadrant,
Sutton,
Surrey, SM2 5AS

Computing Today,
Argus Specialist Publications Ltd,
1 Golden Square,
London, W1R 3AB

Commodore Computing International,
Computabits,
167–169 Great Portland Street,
London, W1

Computer Bulletin,
John Wiley & Sons Ltd,
Baffins Lane,
Chichester,
Sussex, PO19 1UD

Computer News,
The Publishing Company,
99 Grays Inn Road,
London, WC1

The Computer Journal,
John Wiley & Sons Ltd,
Baffins Lane,
Chichester,
Sussex, PO19 1UD

Computer Survey,
United Trade Press Ltd,
UTP House,
33–35 Bowling Green Lane,
London, EC1

Computer Weekly,
Electrical-Electronic Press,
Quadrant House,
The Quadrant,
Sutton,
Surrey, SM2 5AS

Data Processing,
Butterworth Scientific Ltd,
PO Box 63,
Westbury House,
Bury Street,
Guildford,
Surrey, GU2 5BH

Electronics and Computing Monthly,
Scriptor Court,
156 Farringdon Road,
London, EC1R 3AD

Home Computing Weekly,
Argus Specialist Publications Ltd,
1 Golden Square,
London, W1R 3AB

The IBM System User,
EMAP Business and Computer Publications Ltd,
Petersham House,
57A Hatton Garden,
London, EC1

Irish Computer,
"Birchdale",
Cherrywood Road,
Loughlinstown,
Co. Dublin

Infoworld,
Popular Computing Inc.,
Suite 303,
530 Lytton Avene,
Palo Alfo,
California, CA 94301,
U.S.A.

Microbusiness,
Electrical–Electronic Press,
Quadrant House,
The Quadrant,
Sutton,
Surrey, SM2 5AS

Micro,
Micro Ink, Inc.,
10 Northern Boulevard,
Amherst,
New Hampshire, NH 03031,
U.S.A.

Microchoice,
Argus Specialist Publications Ltd,
1 Golden Square,
London, W1R 3AB

Microcomputer News,
Microcomputer News Ltd,
Cromwell House,
20 Bride Lane,
London, EC4Y 8DX

Micro-Scope,
Sportscene Specialist Press Ltd,
14 Rathbone Place,
London, W1P 1DE

Minicomputer,
Compass Press Ltd,
Cromwell House,
20 Bride Lane,
London, EC4Y 8DX

Personal Computer News,
Computing Publications Ltd,
62 Oxford Street,
London, W1A 2HG

Personal Computer World,
Computing Publications Ltd,
62 Oxford Street,
London, W1A 2HG

Personal Computing Today,
Argus Specialist Publications Ltd,
1 Golden Square,
London, W1R 3AB

Personal Software,
Argus Specialist Publications Ltd,
1 Golden Square,
London, W1R 3AB

Popular Computing Weekly,
Sunshine Publications Ltd,
12–13 Little Newport Street,
London, WC2R 3LD

Practical Computing,
Electrical-Electronic Press,
Quadrant House,
The Quadrant,
Sutton,
Surrey, SM2 5AS

QL User,
Database Publications Ltd,
68 Chester Road,
Hazel Grove,
Stockport,
Greater Manchester, SK7 5NY

Soft,
Sportscene Specialist Press Ltd,
14 Rathbone Place,
London, W1P 1DE

Softalk,
Softalk Publishing Co.,
11160 McCormick Street,
North Hollywood,
California, CA 91603,
U.S.A.

Software,
Electrical-Electronic Press,
Quadrant House,
The Quadrant,
Sutton,
Surrey, SM2 5AS

Software File,
EMAP Business & Computer Publications Ltd,
151 Farringdon Road,
London, EC1

Software Index,
IPC Magazines Ltd,
Westover House,
West Quay Road,
Poole,
Dorset

What Micro,
VNU Business Publications BV,
Evelyn House,
62 Oxford Street,
London, W1A 2HG

What's New In Computing,
Morgan–Grampian plc,
Morgan–Grampian House,
30 Calderwood Street,
London, SE18 6QH

What Computer?,
EMAP Business & Computer Publications,
Durrant House,
8 Herbal Hill,
London, EC1R 5JB

Which Computer?,
EMAP Business and Computer Publications Ltd,
Durrant House,
8 Herbal Hill,
London, EC1R 5JB

Which Micro? and Software Review,
EMAP Business & Computer Publications Ltd,
Scriptor Court,
Farringdon Road,
London, EC1

S.A. Amateur Computing,
Nasionale Computer Publications,
PO Box 13138,
Sir Lowry Road 7960,
Cape Town,
South Africa

S.A. MicroComputer Owner,
Systems Publishers (Pty) Ltd,
388 Jan Smuts Avenue,
Craighall Park,
Johannesburg,
South Africa

Australian Personal Computing,
77 Glenhuntly Road,
Elwood Vic. 3184,
Australia

Your Computer Magazine,
140 Joynton Avenue,
Waterloo NSW 2017,
Australia

Micro World Magazine & Australian Computer World Magazine,
37 Alexander Street,
Crows Nest NSW 2065,
Australia

Pacific Computer Weekly,
73 Commonwealth Street,
Sydney NSW 2000,
Australia

Interface Magazine,
17 George Street,
Newmarket,
Auckland,
New Zealand

Bits & Bytes Magazine,
P.O. Box 827,
Christchurch,
New Zealand

Systems Digest,
73 Great North Road,
Grey Lynn,
Auckland,
New Zealand

GLOSSARY

AFTER-SALES SUPPORT
The attention that a seller pays to the user after the sale is made is after-sales support. In programming, this includes the correction of "bugs" and providing updates when available.

BIT
A bit is the basic unit of information in a computer, usually represented by a one or a zero. A combination of 8 bits is called a **byte** which usually represents one computer character. Computer memories are measured in bytes or number of characters.

COMPILER LANGUAGE
These are languages that when executed translate the entire program only once into computer-readable code, after which the program can be loaded, linked to other programs, and executed any number of times without retranslation. Some languages can be translated by either a compiler or interpreter. (See **Interpretive Language**.)

CPU
An abbreviation for Central Processing Unit, this is the heart of a computer processing system. It has the memory and logic to operate the entire system including such peripherals as the printer, disk drives, keyboard and monitor display. It is also sometimes called the systems unit.

DATABASE SYSTEM
A computer-based record keeping system that usually provides for the establishment of data input screen formats, the manipulation of files, and preparation of reports based on selected criteria and format.

DISK DRIVE

Like a small record player, a disk drive rotates a plastic-based disk, commonly 5¼ inches in diameter, and writes and reads the data recorded on the disk (or diskette) by means of a recording head that comes in contact with the diskette. (See **Floppy Disk** and **Hard Disk**.)

DISKETTE

See **Floppy Disk**.

DOCUMENTATION

This is the written material accompanying computer hardware and software that explains its operation, provides examples of its use, and outlines what to do in case of errors.

DOT-MATRIX PRINTER

This printer forms its characters by means of closely spaced dots. The dot matrix is usually a rectangle 7 dots wide and 9 dots high, but this may vary by make. The quality of the print is generally inferior to the **Letter-Quality Printer**, although the speed is usually higher.

FLOPPY DISK

A thin, flexible plastic disk coated with magnetic recording material, the floppy disk is used to store information for later reading. Floppy disks for personal computers are both single- and double-sided and have storage capacities in the hundreds of thousands of bytes or characters. Floppy disks are inserted into the disk drive for reading or writing and are removed and stored when not in use.

HARD DISKS

These are disk drives that generally use nonremovable disks (unlike the floppy disks) but hold many times the data stored on floppies. Hard disks today usually start in the 5 million byte storage range and go upwards to 20 or 30 million bytes, or 20 or 30 MEGS (millions of bytes).

HARDWARE

This term refers to all the computer equipment except the programs needed to run the computer. It includes such items as the systems unit or CPU, the disk drives, keyboard, printers, and all the other equipment needed to operate a computer.

HIGH-LEVEL LANGUAGE
A programming language, the "high-level" means that its statements are close to grammatically correct English, making it relatively easy to read and write. Examples of high-level languages include COBOL and BASIC.

HORIZONTAL MARKETING
Marketing the same product or service across industry lines is horizontal marketing. This is opposed to vertical marketing where a product or service is offered and is useful to only one industry. An example is an accounts system used by many companies in differing fields.

INTERPRETIVE LANGUAGE
This type of language translates and executes a program one statement at a time, each time the program is run. Compare this with compiler language, noted above.

LETTER-QUALITY PRINTER
A printer of this kind forms its characters by use of conventional typewriter character typebars or "daisy wheels". The quality of print is usually superior to that of a dot-matrix printer, noted above.

MODEM
An abbreviation for modulator-demodulator, it is a piece of equipment that attaches to your computer through a cable and takes computer-generated signals and makes them suitable for transmission over telephone lines.

MONITOR
This is the cathode ray tube (CRT) device attached to a computer for the display of input and output information. Some use television sets for monitors but the television image is generally of lower quality than the manufacturer supplied monitor. Monitors are both monochrome and colour.

OBJECT CODE
When the computer translates programming code, either by compilers or interpreters, it translates the code into a format that the computer can understand. This format is called the object code.

OFF-LINE
A generic term, this indicates that a process is not connected to the main computer activity. It sometimes connotes an activity that will provide support to the main operation at a later time.

ON-LINE
The opposite of off-line, on-line means that an activity is connected with the main computer operation and sometimes is used to indicate immediate reaction of the computer system to inputs as opposed to delayed reaction from off-line inputs.

OPERATING SYSTEM
This is the program that coordinates the entire operation of the computer and all its components and also provides user access to the computer. On some systems this is called a disk operating system since it provides for the flow of data between the CPU and the disk drives.

PORTABILITY
This term refers to the ease with which a program written in a particular language to run on one computer can be run on another. High portability means little or no changes to a program are necessary to run on another system; low portability means substantial changes are required.

REMARK LINES
These lines of code in a program do not affect its execution but provide explanatory material about the program's operation.

SERVICE BUREAU
As used in the computer field, this means a computer resource operated by its owners to provide computer services to others. The users generally bring the inputs to the service bureau where the processing is done by the operators; the output is then returned to the users.

SOFTWARE

All the programs used to operate a computer make up the software. This includes the operating systems, application programs, and utilities. Basically, it is everything that is not hardware.

SOURCE CODE

These are the program statements written by a programmer in a language he can understand. This source code is then translated into object code that the computer can understand either by compilers or interpreters.

SPREAD-SHEET PROGRAM

A class of software that simulates the classical accounting spread sheet of rows and columns, this has the added capability of establishing relationships among the rows and columns so that any changes are reflected in the related row or column.

SYSTEM-LEVEL FLOW DIAGRAMS

These are diagrams that depict the flow of information in a computer system at the file and processing level, not at the detailed programming logic level. System-level flow diagrams precede program diagrams in the normal application development.

SYSTEMS HOUSE

This is a company that provides an entire computer application installation: hardware, software and training. The complete installation is sometimes called a "turnkey" since the end user simply "turns a key" and begins processing his data.

TEMPLATE

As used in the computer system sense, a template is a program that is used in conjunction with another program to provide an enhanced capability. The template program is overlaid on the main program to establish a more powerful system.

TURNKEY SYSTEM
See **Systems House**.

USER FRIENDLY

The characteristic of a computer program to provide easy-to-follow instructions and reject errors in a way to allow the user to continue processing easily.

UTILITY PROGRAMS

This is a class of software that helps other software perform better or aids programmers to work more efficiently. An example is spoolers that allow the computer to print while processing data.

VENDOR SUPPORT

This is similar to after-sales support, noted above, but could include other things such as training programs, onsite repair service, and knowledgeable personnel.

INDEX

A

Accounting, 28, 57, 60, 67–68, 92, 119–120
Advertising, 22, 25, 40, 44, 49; consultant's, 103, 104–105; learning from, 95; systems houses, 114–115
Answering services, 28
Appearance, 25, 103
Apple computers, 31
Applications programming, 32
Assembly language, 137

B

BASIC, 34, 136, 137
Bentley, Nelson, 42
Bookkeeping systems, 119–120
Business cards, 25, 27, 105, 114

C

Commodore, 31
Compatibility of computers, 20
Computer acquisition methods, 35–36
Computers, choice of, 29–31
Computer stores, 95, 115
Computer-to-computer communication, 34
Conflict of interest, 17
Consulting, 14, 20, 64, 80, 90–106, 134; reports, 99–100
Contract programming, 80–89, 132
Contracts, 28, 84, 102, 106, 127–128
Copyright, 78–79, 85; service

bureau, 61
Copy writing, 40, 49
Corporations, 123–124
Costs, 31–32
CP/M, 32

D

Database systems, 33
Data error, 63–64
Data processing operations, 56
Deadlines, 25, 26, 42–43, 59, 63, 82
Deductions, tax, 125–126, 127
Depreciation, 126
Direct mail, 105
Discretion, need for, 15–17
Documentation of programs, 50–51, 71–72, 74, 95–96, 139–140

E

Editing, 42
Educational games, 77
Educational opportunities, 24
Educational programs, 67, 68
Equipment selection, 29–31
Expertise, development of, 19

F

FORTH, 137, 138
FORTRAN, 137, 138
Freelance writing, 38–53, 131

G

Games, 67, 68; educational, 77

T

Tax considerations, 28, 125–7
Tax preparation, 13, 57, 61, 62, 75–76
Tax returns, 29, 118, 120, 122–125
Technical writing, 39, 44, 50–51
Telephone answering machines, 28
Time management, 26
Time rental, 58
Trade journals, 22
Training manuals, 44

Travel agencies, 93
TRS computers, 31, 32
Turnkey systems, 108–117

W

Warranties, 61, 116
Wholesalers, 92
Wirth, Nicklaus, 137
Word processing, 56, 62, 67, 68
Writer's guides, 45, 47
Writing, freelance, 38–53, 131